# HOLY WEEK

# Holy Week

## A SERIES OF MEDITATIONS

ST VLADIMIR'S SEMINARY PRESS
YONKERS NEW YORK 2018

LIBRARY OF CONGRESS CATALOGING-IN-PUBLICATION DATA

Title: Holy Week : a series of meditations.
Description: Yonkers, NY : St. Vladimirs Seminary Press, 2018.
Includes bibliographical references.
Identifiers: LCCN 2017057728 (print) | LCCN 2017058745 (ebook)
ISBN 9780881416145 | ISBN 9780881416138 (alk. paper)
Subjects: LCSH: Holy Week—Meditations. | Orthodox Eastern
Church—Doctrines.
Classification: LCC BX376.35.H64 (ebook) | LCC BX376.35.H64 H6 2018
(print) | DDC 242/.35—dc23
LC record available at https://lccn.loc.gov/2017057728

ST VLADIMIR'S SEMINARY PRESS
575 Scarsdale Road, Yonkers, New York, 10707
1-800-204-2665 | svspress.com

ISBN 978–0–88141–613-8 (paper)
ISBN 978–0–88141–614-5 (electronic)



Book cover & interior design:
Amber Schley Iragui

PRINTED IN THE UNITED STATES OF AMERICA

*The publication of this book*
*was made possible by a generous donation from*
DR DONALD J. TAMULONIS, JR.
*in honor of his grandsons*
*Jack Thomas Wysmier & Reid Daniel Wysmier*
*and all children as they begin*
*their lifelong journey*
*in the Orthodox faith.*

# Contents

## HOLY TUESDAY



## HOLY WEDNESDAY



## HOLY THURSDAY



## HOLY FRIDAY

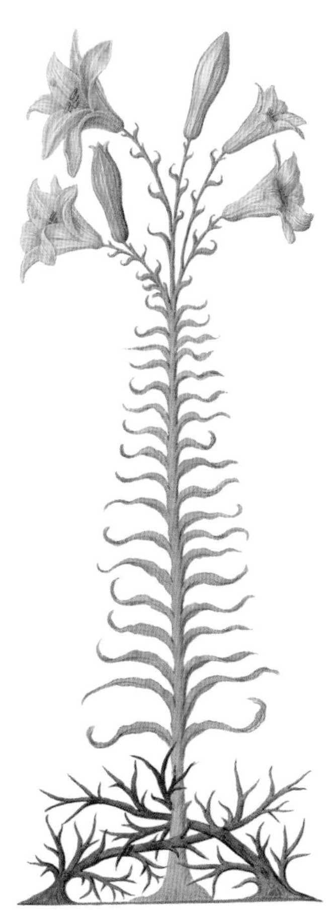

IC XC

# LAZARUS SATURDAY

# 1

ARCHPRIEST CHAD HATFIELD

# Resurrection and the Faith of Children

## RESURRECTION AS CENTRAL TO CHURCH LIFE

The words of the Apostle Paul beautifully underscore the centrality of the Resurrection within the Orthodox Christian faith:

> *Now if Christ is preached that he has been raised from the dead, how do some among you say that there is no resurrection of the dead? But if there is no resurrection of the dead, then*

*Christ is not risen. And if Christ is not risen, then our preaching is empty and your faith is also empty.* (1 Cor 15.12–14)

*But now, Christ is risen from the dead and has become the first fruits of those who have fallen asleep. For since by man came death, by Man also came the resurrection of the dead. For as in Adam all die, even so in Christ all shall be made alive.* (1 Cor 15.20–22)

Like St Paul, we Orthodox Christians also affirm our belief in the Resurrection each time we profess our faith with the words of the Nicene Creed. We also rejoice on Pascha as we sing: "Christ is risen from the dead, trampling down death by death, and upon those in the tombs bestowing life." And, we believe firmly that the first fruits mentioned in the Old Testament, given in offering to God (Ex 23.16), are promises of the greater fruits of new life through Christ's rising from the dead (1 Cor 15.20).

Lazarus Saturday offers a unique liturgical affirmation of this centrality; it is the only time outside of Sunday that we celebrate a "resurrection" service. On this day we shout that Christ Jesus has raised Lazarus, confirming the universal resurrection of humanity—even before his own passion, death, and Resurrection:

*By raising Lazarus from the dead before your Passion,*
*Thou didst confirm the universal resurrection, O Christ God!*
*Like the children with branches of victory, we cry out to thee,*
*O Vanquisher of Death: "Hosanna in the highest!*
*Blessed is he that comes in the name of the Lord!"*

—Troparion of the Feast

The narrative of Lazarus Saturday assures us: the Evil One had given his best shot, but as Lazarus is called forth from his tomb, the devil's best was not good enough to stand against the Love of God. On this day, Hades surely trembles as it anticipates the Lord himself descending into its very depths.

## RESURRECTION IN SCRIPTURE, IMAGERY, AND THE CHURCH FATHERS

In addition to the resurrection of Lazarus, the New Testament notes two other occasions where a person is restored to life by the Lord.[1] St Mark records the raising of Jairus's daughter (Mk 5.21–24, 35–43), and St Luke records the raising of the son of the Widow of Nain (Lk 7.11–17). In the first story, we see Jesus touch the little girl,

The Raising of Jairus' Daughter, William Blake.

and we hear him speak in Aramaic: "Talitha, cumi," which means, "Little girl, I say to you, arise." In the second story, Jesus touches not the boy himself, but rather, his coffin. In these three resurrection stories, we see a progression: from Jesus touching a child, to Jesus touching only a coffin, to Jesus touching nothing at all but instead using his voice to summon the dead back to life; and all of creation hears his command: "Lazarus, come forth!" and "Loose him, and let him go." Lazarus comes forth in his shroud (unlike our Lord, who leaves his shroud behind after his Resurrection)—as he will someday need his burial clothes again!

However, the concept of resurrection is not limited to the pages of the New Testament. Our Christian belief in the Resurrection stems from Judaism itself. For Jews, Hades, a place of shades, is a kind of "holding pen" where contact with the living and God himself is suspended (Ps 6.5). Some Old Testament figures, such as Enoch and Elijah, are simply "taken up" to heaven, avoiding Hades and death altogether. Many Christian commentators have interpreted these events from "this side" of the Resur-

The Raising of Lazarus, Hunterian Psalter.

rection, as prophecies of what is to come, looking forward to the general resurrection: "for the hour is coming in which all who are in the graves will hear his voice and come forth—those who have done good, to the resurrection of life, and those who have done evil, to the resurrection of condemnation" (Jn 5.28–29).

So powerful was his Resurrection that he was the cause of resurrection for others as well.

From Scripture, we know that the Pharisees and Sadducees differed greatly on the Jewish teaching regarding the resurrection. We read in the Book of Acts:

> *Now as they spoke to the people, the priests, the captain of the temple, and the Sadducees came upon them, being greatly disturbed that they taught the people and preached in Jesus the resurrection from the dead. And they laid hands on them, and put them in custody until the next day, for it was already evening. However, many of those who heard the word believed; and the number of men came to be about five thousand.* (Acts 4.1–4)

The great preacher, St John Chrysostom, reflected on this same passage:

> *They were annoyed, not only because the apostles were teaching, but because they declared that not only was Jesus Christ himself risen from the dead but that through him we too rise again.... So powerful was his Resurrection that he is the cause of resurrection for others as well.*[2]

> The Feast of Saint Lazarus marks a time of transition. On the eve of Lazarus Saturday the Great Fast ends, but Great and Holy Week has not yet begun.

Thus, Holy Scripture and the Holy Fathers testify to the importance of the Resurrection.

Likewise, the Orthodox Christian tradition is replete with images of the *Anastasis* (lit., "Resurrection"). In many of these iconographic depictions, Hades is bound as Christ takes the hand of Adam and pulls him from the pit of darkness and isolation. The powerful, personal encounter with the resurrected Lord, reflected in such imagery, gives the Church its firm foundation—a foundation upon which the Canon of New Testament Scripture and the Nicene Creed rest. Indeed, an encounter with the risen person of Christ fuels the ascetic life lived by each Christian as he or she experiences new life and prepares for eternal life beyond the grave.

On Lazarus Saturday, we believers also encounter the power of resurrection, wrought by our Lord. We rejoice as we hear the voice of Jesus calling forth Lazarus, four days dead!

## RESURRECTION AS A FEAST OF TRANSITION

The Feast of St Lazarus marks a time of transition. On the eve of Lazarus Saturday the Great Fast ends, but Great and Holy Week has not yet begun.

The Church placed the feast at this point in the liturgical calendar because it "serves as a necessary 'rest' and 'transition' between the rigors of the Fast and the awesome and saving events of Holy Week. For in truth, yesterday evening's Vespers not only ended the Holy Forty Days, but also ushered us into a joyous resurrectional prelude that will eventually lead to our Savior's Passion."[2]

Interestingly, the Spanish nun Egeria—who kept an extensive travel diary noting liturgical practices in the Levant and Jerusalem between AD 381–384—records Lazarus Saturday as a joyful celebration: it was the last day of instruction for catechumens who were preparing for Christian initiation rites.[3] The catechumens now would transition into being full communicants in Christ's Church, beginning by participating in the rigors of the week of Christ's Passion.

## OUT OF THE MOUTHS OF BABES

We adults try to rationalize the reality of the Resurrection; our mental contortions belie the simple faith of children—a faith that models fruit-bearing discipleship. On Lazarus Saturday, our eyes

The Raising of Lazarus, detail.

see the joy of children as they behold the Resurrection and rejoice in something they cannot explain, but acknowledge by faith to be true. Their joy is augmented by many liturgical customs involving children, which have developed throughout the centuries and which highlight Jesus' friends: Lazarus, and his sisters Martha and Mary.

One such custom is based on a popular Middle Eastern legend that claims St Lazarus (who later became bishop of Citium in Cypress), after being raised from the dead, only ate sweet-tasting foods, as a sign of joy in having had a foretaste of the sweetness of eternal life in Christ. In places that have received this ancient story, the children of a parish, in an outdoor procession following the Divine Liturgy, re-enter the church by passing under a branch, upon which special lenten sweet treats have been tied. As the children pass under the branch, they pull off these treats and eat them—and they remember St Lazarus!

*Ernesta,* Cecilia Beaux.

In Romania on Lazarus Saturday, especially in Wallachia, a young girl is chosen to dress in bridal clothing, signifying anticipation of the wedding feast that will be enjoyed by all believers in the general resurrection. Then she and her companion girls trek through their villages, dancing and singing of St Lazarus. Specially baked breads are also given to the children and the needy, and flowers are planted in preparation for Holy Pascha.

Whatever ethnic or local custom you observe on Lazarus Saturday, take special note of the children.

Serbian Orthodox Christians keep the custom of *Vrbica*, or "Little Willows." Children go into the woods to find pussy willows, and bring them back to their parish for a procession; they sing the festal Troparion, as if they were going with Christ to the tomb of Lazarus. Additionally, they dress in their very best clothes, as if it were already Pascha, and they bring bells to church on Lazarus Saturday, making a "holy noise."

Whatever ethnic or local custom you observe on Lazarus Saturday, take special note of the children. How many of us have had our hearts melt when seeing the excitement on the faces of our children as they carry homemade candles in procession for Lazarus Saturday, or have had our own faith renewed as we hearing their excited voices telling us of the coming celebration of Holy Pascha? Our children model perfect faith for those of us who have made our faith too complicated to enjoy the simple truth: Christ is risen!

Give children their place on this day, and ponder once again Jesus' key words:

> *At that time the disciples came to Jesus, saying, "Who then is greatest in the kingdom of heaven?" Then Jesus called a little child to him, set him in the midst of them and said, "Assuredly, I say to you, unless you are converted and become as little children, you will by no means enter the kingdom of heaven. Therefore, whoever humbles himself as this little child is the greatest in the kingdom of heaven. Whoever receives one little child like this in my name receives me."* (Mt 18.1–5)

On Palm Sunday, the children of the Hebrews ran to greet the Messiah, spreading branches and palms along the way as he entered Jerusalem on a colt. When we see our children rejoicing and having fun on Lazarus Saturday and on Palm Sunday—perhaps waving palms and shouting "Hosanna!"—then remember the words of Jesus to his disciples: "Let the little children come to me, and do not forbid them; for of such is the kingdom of heaven" (Mt 19.14).

## ABOUT THE AUTHOR

**Very Rev. Chad Hatfield**, D.Min., D.D. is President of St Vladimir's Orthodox Theological Seminary, and the former President of St Herman Theological Seminary in Kodiak, Alaska. He has many years of pastoral experience in parish and missionary work, and continues to contribute to the fields of missiology and pastoral theology. He is the editor of the Orthodox Profiles and Orthodoxy and Missions series at St Vladimir's Seminary Press.

# PALM SUNDAY

2

ARCHPRIEST J. SERGIUS HALVORSEN

# Victory of the Heart

*Hosanna! Blessed is he who comes in the name of the Lord. Hosanna in the highest!* (Mk 11.9–10)

Today Jesus enters into Jerusalem, and the cheering crowd greets him like a king entering the city after a military victory—the first-century equivalent of a "ticker tape parade." The crowd has heard about Jesus, about his powerful teaching and his miracles, and specifically, his miracle of raising Lazarus from the dead.

They cry out, "Hosanna in the highest," a shout of praise and a plea for salvation that literally means "Save us, Lord!" For years, for generations, these people have languished under the heavy boot of Roman occupation and oppression. They are weary of high taxes, soldiers in their streets, and the constant threat of violence. The people are tired and weary and hungry, and they want freedom.

> Standing with our palm branches today, singing, "Hosanna in the highest," we stand shoulder to shoulder with our first-century brothers & sisters, longing for freedom.

Do you ever feel that way?

## THE DESIRE FOR FREEDOM

Today in some parts of the world Christians struggle under the heavy yoke of political oppression and military occupation. In some places Christians are in the middle of military conflict and civil war. But, even people who enjoy great political freedom—like we do in the United States—can feel this sense of soul-crushing oppression. We can be oppressed by strained relationships among family and friends. We can be oppressed by the anxiety and stress of economic uncertainty. We can be oppressed by the agony of addiction. We can be oppressed by the pain and grief of illness and death.

And wherever there is oppression, there is a powerful desire for freedom. We may not face oppression from the Roman Empire, but standing with our palm branches today, singing, "Hosanna in the highest," we stand shoulder to shoulder with our first-century brothers and sisters, longing for freedom. But how do we get freedom? How do we obtain liberation from our physical, emotional, and spiritual oppression? The obvious answer is: *go out and fight for it.*

This was what the crowd in Jerusalem wanted from Jesus as he traveled on that "red carpet" of palm branches and the clothes off their backs (Mk 11.8). In their eyes, Jesus was the perfect man to lead a righteous rebellion. Surely God's anointed could raise up an army and restore the kingdom of Israel. After all, if Jesus had the power to raise Lazarus from the dead, he would be invincible in the face of Roman legions. If Jesus was truly God's Anointed One, then he would be invincible in battle. The crowd wanted the kind of freedom that you win with the spear, the chariot, and the sword.

But to win that kind of freedom you need wealth, strength, and power. Those sound awfully good, don't they? With money, a strong body, and political influence, freedom is yours for the taking... Or is it?

Battle scene, detail.

## THE PRICE OF FREEDOM

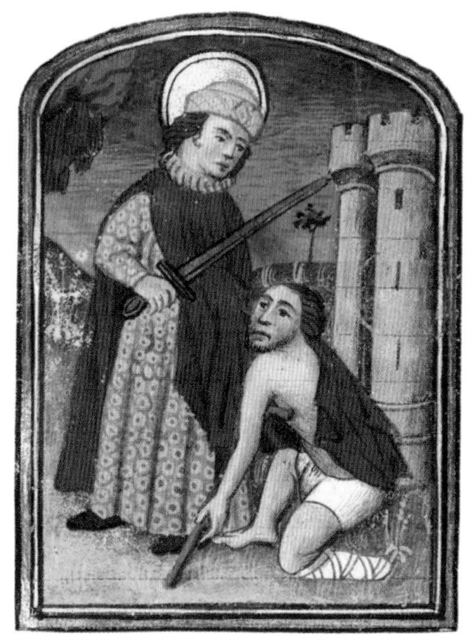

St Martin shares his cloak with a beggar, prayer book.

Ancient Israel had great power, but fell to the Babylonians. In Jesus' time the Roman Empire had great power, but over the centuries that empire fell to other nations. It's undeniable: as one nation rises, other nations fight to gain supremacy.

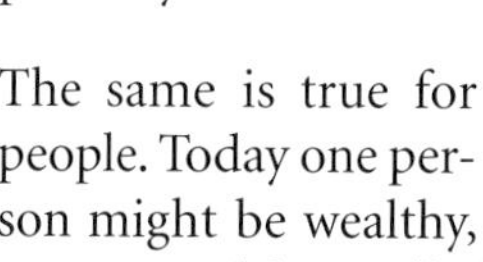

The same is true for people. Today one person might be wealthy, strong, and have all the power in the world. But one who gains worldly power quickly becomes a target for everyone else who wants a place at the top of the food chain.

And so, strength, wealth, and power come with a terrible price. They come with fear, isolation, and anxiety. The more we possess of this world, the more this world will try to take away. So we prepare for battle, we harden our defenses and sharpen our attacks. Whether we attack others with swords or words, with bullets or with business savvy, we strike others where they are weakest, where we can do the greatest amount of damage and gain the greatest advantage.

The crowd was hungry for power, and they hoped that Jesus would lead them to victory in an epic battle that would change their world. On a certain level, the crowd was right. They were at the threshold of a great battle that would change everything—a battle that would grant freedom to the oppressed and vanquish the foe.

However, the army that Jesus came to fight was not flesh and blood; it was, as St Paul says, a battle against the "spiritual hosts of wickedness in the heavenly places" (Eph 6.12). And this battle had begun long before Jesus entered into Jerusalem.

> Whether we attack others with swords or words, with bullets or with business savvy, we strike others where they are weakest, where we can do the greatest amount of damage and gain the greatest advantage.

## THE PATH TO FREEDOM

After Jesus was baptized in the Jordan River, he went out into the wilderness and fasted for forty days. After that long fast, the tempter comes and tempts Jesus.

"You are hungry? If you are the Son of God, command those stones to become loaves of bread," says the evil one. This is not merely a temptation about food. Satan is tempting Jesus with wealth. If Jesus were to turn stones into bread, he would never go hungry. And if one were to possess an unlimited supply of bread, he could have virtually unlimited wealth. But Jesus launches a counter-attack and replies, "It is written, 'Man shall not live by bread alone, but by every word that proceeds from the mouth of God'" (Mt 4.4).

Then the tempter takes Jesus to the Holy City, sets him on the top of the Temple, and says, "If you are the Son of God, throw yourself down; for it is written, 'He will give his angels charge of you,' and 'On their hands they will bear you up, lest you strike your foot against a stone'" (Mt 4.6). Satan tempts Jesus with strength, with physical invincibility. "If you are *really* the Son of God, then you can do anything, even jump off a cliff, and you'll be fine." According to this demonic logic, not only could Jesus perform super human feats, but he also would be physically invulnerable. He could literally live forever, doing anything he pleased in this world. The spiritual battle becomes more intense, and Christ replies, "Again it is written, 'You shall not tempt the Lord your God'" (Mt 4.7).

The Temptation of Christ by the devil, Hunterian Psalter.

Finally, Satan takes Jesus up to the top of a high mountain, shows him all of the kingdoms of the world and points out all the glory of all those kingdoms, and he says, "All these I will give you, if you will fall down and worship me" (Mt 4.9). It is the ultimate offer of power. What would it be like to rule over the entire world, over all its kingdoms and all its peoples, and have access to all its wealth and all its pleasures? At some level, Jesus must have known that all of this could be his: perfect strength, infinite wealth, and limitless power. Yet, he strikes a powerful blow against the powers of wickedness in his reply: "Be gone, Satan! For it is written, 'You shall worship the Lord your God and him only shall you serve'" (Mt 4.10).

Today, on Palm Sunday, we have fasted forty days, we are hungry, and if ever we face temptation from Satan, it is now. We face the temptation to gratify ourselves with worldly delights. We face the temptation to demand our liberty from everything and everyone that oppresses us. We face the temptation to fight for strength, and wealth, and power. This is the spiritual warfare that constantly rages on all sides, and today on Palm Sunday the battle is particularly violent.

Today, on Palm Sunday, we have fasted forty days, we are hungry, and if ever we face temptation from Satan, it is now.

As Jesus enters Jerusalem, he faces these temptations as never before—all of those people cheering, crying out "Hosanna!," just begging him to be their worldly general, their commander, their emperor. Yet Christ refuses to be the earthly king that the people demand. Instead he will be revealed as a kind of king that the world has never seen, a perfect king, a heavenly king, a humble king, crowned with thorns, robed in the purple of mockery, and enthroned on the Cross. Though Christ enters Jerusalem and is enveloped in a fire storm of temptation, he keeps his eyes on the Cross. *This is the victory of Palm Sunday.*

Today as well, Jesus Christ enters into the Jerusalem of our hearts to lead us to victory. Today, Christ fills us with his power, his strength, and his resolve to overcome the temptation to worldly power. For "the Son of man came not to be served but to serve, and to give his life as a ransom for many" (Mt 20.28).

Christ refuses to be the earthly king that the people demand. Instead he will be revealed as a kind of king that the world has never seen... a humble king, crowned with thorns, robed in mockery, and enthroned on the Cross.

And so today we also cry out, "Hosanna in the highest!," for Christ vanquishes the powers of evil, and through his perfect sacrifice on the Cross we are liberated from the oppressive desire for worldly power. Christ leads us to the unexpected victory in which the King lays down his own life for the salvation of all.

The entry of Christ into Jerusalem, English psalter.

In his dying, the true majesty and power of the Lord is perfectly revealed and the powers of hell are vanquished.

Following Christ, we lay down our lives as he did: for our brothers and sisters, our neighbor, and even our enemy. Today we cry out, "Hosanna in the highest!" as we follow our Lord to his voluntary Passion and death on the Cross.

## ABOUT THE AUTHOR

**Archpriest J. Sergius Halvorsen**, the Director of the Doctor of Ministry Program and the Assistant Professor of Homiletics and Rhetoric at St Vladimir's Seminary, is currently working on a volume in homiletics. He contributes regularly to *The Preacher*, a publication of The College of Preachers, Nottingham, UK.

# HOLY MONDAY

3

PRIEST GEORGE L. PARSENIOS

# Joseph, the Noble Patriarch, and Biblical Interpretation as a Way of Life

We interpret the Bible in many ways. We give homilies and write commentaries. We sing hymns and lead Bible studies. And when we interpret the Bible, we wrestle with ancient languages and struggle in many other ways to draw forth the meaning of the text.

But in addition to all of our homilies and hymns and beyond all our commentaries and our Bible Studies lies another form of biblical interpretation. And it brings a different struggle.

It is the not the struggle to translate or to explain the Gospel. It is the struggle to live the Gospel. Here we do not grapple with ancient languages, but with our very selves—our habits, our sins, our every instinct that leads us away from God. We struggle to rise above our limitations and our mistakes in order to make the Gospel shine forth in our lives. The Apostle Paul announces, "It is no longer I who live, but Christ who lives in me" (Gal 2.20). To look at Paul is to see the Gospel message of Christ in human form. It is to the see the Gospel interpreted in a living icon of Christ.

To live the Gospel is not easy. We need help along the way. We need models to imitate. This is why Paul says, "Be imitators of me, as I am of Christ" (1Cor 11.1). The difficulty in imitating either St Paul or any other saint from history, though, is that they are no longer walking and talking before our eyes. We struggle to imitate what we cannot even see.

Here we do not grapple with ancient languages, but with our very selves—our habits, our sins, our every instinct that leads us away from God.

The Church recognizes this dilemma and provides us with vivid models to imitate, in the visible form of icons and the written lives of the saints—but even more so in the Church's hymns. Our hymns, of course, have many purposes. Sometimes they are hymns of praise and sometimes they express a profound theological message. Over and above these purposes, our hymns also offer a rich collection of living, breathing models for imitation, and these models help us to shape ourselves into living, breathing interpretations of the Gospel message.

The hymns of Holy Week are a treasure house of such models. We see biblical characters put on stage before our eyes, acting out the events of Christ's Passion. Different characters are presented to us on the different nights of the week. Some of them we are encouraged to follow, others we are supposed to reject.

The sinful woman anoints Christ's feet with her tears, English psalter.

For instance, on Holy Tuesday we see the figures of Judas and the sinful woman who anointed Christ's feet with her tears. The sinful woman is a model of repentance to follow, while Judas is a model of betrayal to avoid. By hearing and seeing these biblical characters act out the drama of Holy Week, we too are drawn up into the drama. We are not just spectators, but actors on the stage of the Christian life. At each and every service, we do not merely observe the events of the Crucifixion and Resurrection. We are ourselves dying and rising with Christ.

On Holy Monday the twin images put before our eyes are the fig tree cursed by Christ (Mt 21.19) and the noble person of Joseph. The image we should imitate is Joseph, the Old Testament Patriarch (Gen 37–50). Joseph was left for dead by his jealous brothers and then sold into bondage. After trials of many kinds he became a royal official in Egypt, where he was able to save his brothers and all Israel from a great famine. He suffered unjustly at the hands of his brothers but was able to save them through his suffering. He thus typifies the life of Christ, who saved his people through unjust suffering.

But Joseph is not only important because he prefigures the life of Christ. He is also set before us as a model to follow in our own lives.

Jesus curses the fig tree, Arabic Gospel.

The service of Holy Monday focuses on several parts of Joseph's life and work, but especially on the episode in the house of Potiphar, the chief of Pharaoh's guard. After being enslaved and sold into bondage, Joseph was eventually bought by Potiphar. When Potiphar's wife seduced Joseph, Joseph refused to be led into sin. He ran so quickly from Potiphar's house that he fled naked from the house (Gen 39.1–20).

The *Kontakion* and *Oikos* of Holy Monday focus on this episode.

The *Oikos* passage says, "Though enslaved in body, he kept his soul free from bondage." The *Kontakion* reads, "Having spurned the enticements of the Egyptian woman, he was in turn glorified by Him who knows the hearts of men and bestows an incorruptible crown." When tempted, Joseph remained focused on God. Even though he was enslaved by other human beings, he refused to be enslaved by sin.

This is the positive image of Holy Monday. But it is joined to a negative one, the fig tree. We can see how the two images are connected in the final hymns of the night, the *Aposticha*.

The third hymn of the *Aposticha* says, "Mindful of what befell the fig tree, withered for its barrenness, brethren, let us bear fruits worthy of repentance to Christ, who in turn bestows on us great mercy." This hymn is directed specifically toward us. "Mindful," it says, "of what befell the fig tree, let us bear fruits worthy of repentance."

We are not passive spectators. The fig tree is not put before us so that we can feel superior, but as a caution and a reminder to remain vigilant and to bear fruit ourselves.

We are not just watching the drama of Holy Week. We are not passive spectators. The fig tree is not put before us so that we can feel superior to it, or to see others around us as not bearing fruits worthy of repentance. The fig tree is put before us as a caution and a reminder to remain vigilant and to bear fruit ourselves.

Then, immediately following this reference to the tree that bears no fruit, the next hymn turns our attention back to Joseph, as well as to the infamous fruit of another tree, the tree from the Garden of Eden. The hymn says, "Seeing the Egyptian woman as a second Eve, the serpent strove by flattery to cause Joseph's downfall. But he, leaving his tunic behind, fled from sin. And though naked, like our first parent before the fall, he was unashamed."

Joseph is the model Christian who avoids sin and refuses to fall, even when tempted greatly. He is a penitent person, focused on the will of God and focused on removing sin from his life. Because he is a tree that bears good fruit, he avoids the forbidden fruit of sin. The twin images of Joseph and the fig tree are thus joined as opposites.

Joseph accused by Potifer's wife, detail, William Blake.

The *apolytikion* (or *troparion*) from the first several nights of Holy Week makes the same point plain in another set of images. It says, "The Bridegroom sets forth in the middle of the night. And blessed is that servant whom he shall find on watch; unworthy the one he shall come upon sleeping." We must ever be focused on Christ, like the servant who is found watching and not like the servant who is found asleep. On Holy Monday, the fig tree represents the lazy servant found asleep, who does not bear fruits worthy of repentance. Joseph represents the servant found on watch. He does not fall into sin because he is vigilant and prepared.

No less than a sermon or a Bible study, and no less than a long and learned commentary, the hymns of Holy Monday are a form of biblical interpretation, explaining to us the meaning of the fig tree and the significance of the life of Joseph. But they interpret these biblical episodes in a particular way, with the intention of helping the people of God to become living interpretations of the Bible. We see Joseph and other biblical characters put on stage in front of us in the

On Holy Monday, the fig tree represents the lazy servant found asleep and Joseph represents the servant found on watch. Joseph does not fall into sin because he is vigilant and prepared.

drama of Holy Week, not so that we can be passive spectators of what we see, but so that in our own lives we can live the message of the Gospel and say together with the Holy Apostle Paul, "It is no longer I who live, but Christ who lives in me."

## ABOUT THE AUTHOR

**Priest George L. Parsenios**, is Associate Professor of New Testament at Princeton Theological Seminary and Sessional Associate Professor at St Vladimir's Orthodox Theological Seminary. He is a priest in the Greek Orthodox Metropolis of New Jersey.

Abrah

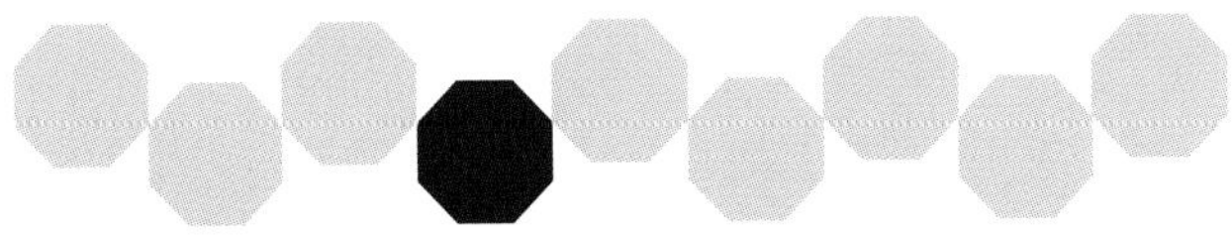

# HOLY TUESDAY

# 4

PROFESSOR PETER C. BOUTENEFF

## A Hymn of Invitation

As we attend and thoughtfully follow the services of Holy Week, we are more and more struck by the incomparably rich hymnography, often sung in unique and evocative melodies. Many of us have favorite hymns, which we greet as friends when they come along each year. There are the landmark hymns of the Bridegroom services, repeated for several nights running. There are, of course, the unforgettable moments of Holy Thursday: the hymn "Of Thy Mystical Supper!" The Twelve Gospels! Then Friday: the Burial Shroud! The Lamentations! Then Saturday: the victorious Prokeimenon! These are like lanterns, lighting our way forward in an otherwise dark terrain.

One of my own favorites is a humbler little hymn (blink and you've missed it for the year!), sung with the Aposticha at Matins and Vespers on Holy Tuesday:

*Come, o faithful,*
*let us work zealously for the Master,*
*for he distributes wealth to his servants.*
*Let each of us, according to his or her ability*
*increase the talent of grace:*
*let one be adorned in wisdom through good works;*
*let another celebrate a service in splendor.*
*The one distributes his wealth to the poor;*
*the other communicates the word to those untaught.*
*Thus we shall increase what has been entrusted to us,*
*and, as faithful stewards of grace,*
*we shall be accounted worthy of the Master's joy.*
*Make us worthy of this, Christ our God,*
*in your love for mankind.*

Why do we sing such a hymn during Holy Week? Let's spend a minute examining its liturgical context, before looking more closely at its words.

Come, O faithful, let us work zealously for the Master!

By the time we sing this hymn, we have already entered squarely into the journey to Christ's life-giving Passion. We have traveled through six weeks of Great Lent. We have celebrated the victorious entry of Our Lord into Jerusalem (a bitter victory:

Jesus knowingly enters the city where he is to be betrayed and slain). We have heard him preaching with increased intensity against civil and religious hypocrisy and injustice. Moreover, as we followed Jesus' journey, we also directed our attention to ourselves, to our own sinful nature and actions.

Through our penitential hymnography (for example, the *Canon of St Andrew of Crete*), we Orthodox Christians apply all the hypocrisy, all the examples of pride, lust, and murderous

Let each of us, according to his or her ability, increase the talent of grace.

The hospitality of Abraham and Sarah to three angels, Danish psalter.

intent, to our own lives as we are living them. It is not a pretty picture of how we live our lives. So we ask God's forgiveness and beg him to help us to become better people.

During Holy Week, our penitence is brought to a high level of intensity, at a dosage that we cannot tolerate for long. But here we are pushed to our limits, because Our Lord himself, the King of Glory, who made the heavens and the earth, is on his way to being betrayed, abandoned, and slaughtered. Matters do not get any more serious than that, so we have to make sure we are paying full attention.

During Holy Week, our penitence is brought to a high level of intensity, at a dosage we cannot tolerate for long.

## WORKING OUT WHAT GOD HAS "WORKED IN"

That is why, at the Bridegroom services, usually celebrated on Sunday, Monday, and Tuesday evenings of Holy Week, we pray for several things surrounding the theme of bringing ourselves into realization of who we are and what is happening:

- We ask God to "illumine the vesture of our souls," to purify us, to give us appropriate spiritual "clothing" in order to celebrate properly the Feast of Feasts.
- We remind ourselves to be wakeful and watchful, we rouse ourselves out of our slumber, to penetrate the usual half-awake state of our minds and hearts.

- We contemplate scriptural images as lessons or feed on them as inspiration. The biblical theme common to all these services is that of the Bridegroom (Christ) who comes in the middle of the night and finds some wedding guests who are prepared, but others who are not, and who cannot be, because of the late hour. On these various evenings we also sing about the withered fig tree, the betrayal of Judas, and—as a positive illustration—the repentant harlot who wipes Jesus' feet with her tears and hair.

Don't *almost* do something; don't think about doing it, don't do it in a half-baked way. Do it and do it well.

Within this broader context, we come to the aforementioned Holy Tuesday hymn, in which we urge each other to do the particular work that God has given us to do. Let's now review what it is saying, and why it may attract us.

- The hymn encourages us to goad each other to work *zealously*: Don't *almost* do something; don't just think about doing it, don't do it in a half-baked way. Do it, and do it well, for the sake of God.

- The hymn reminds us that *God* gives the wedding garment; *God* gives the talent. Without his initial gift, we have nothing, we *are* nothing. But once we realize that God has filled our otherwise empty vessels, it is very much up to us to *take up* his gift, and to *act* on it.

❀ The hymn informs us that when God distributes his gifts, he is not using a cookie cutter to form identically shaped people. He is not drawing a uniform pattern for us to follow, as if we were robots programmed on a set course. We are different from one another; we do not strive to conform to a single model, even if at times, the illustrations of virtuous people within the Church's tradition seem (perhaps frustratingly) uniform—for example, in iconography and spiritual literature, depending on our sources, we might find a preponderance of monks, bishops, and virgin martyrs. But if we look more closely, we will find a message applicable to us as school teachers, social workers, bankers, writers, sanitation workers, and other occupations, as well moms, dads, brothers, and sisters—people in relationships—people from all walks of life.

Wherever we are, whatever we do, whatever our station in life, our task is to build upon what we have been given.

Wherever we are, whatever we do, whatever our station in life, our task is to build upon what we have been given. First, of course, we have to identify our gift, and that is not always simple. But by understanding our gift and recalling that it indeed comes from God himself, we can build on it. The Gospels tell us that wasting our talents is one of the things that seriously displeases God. But we pray that, if we recognize and work with our gifts, we will be "deemed worthy of the Master's joy," a joy that is beyond anything that we can imagine.

Three angels visit Abraham and Sarah, Danish psalter.

## ABOUT THE AUTHOR

**Peter C. Bouteneff** is Professor of Systematic Theology at St Vladimir's Seminary. Additionally, he is Series Editor for the Foundations Series published by St Vladimir's Seminary Press, and author of a volume in that series, *Sweeter than Honey: Orthodox Reflections on Dogma and Truth*. He is also the faculty director for the Sacred Arts Initiative at the Seminary.

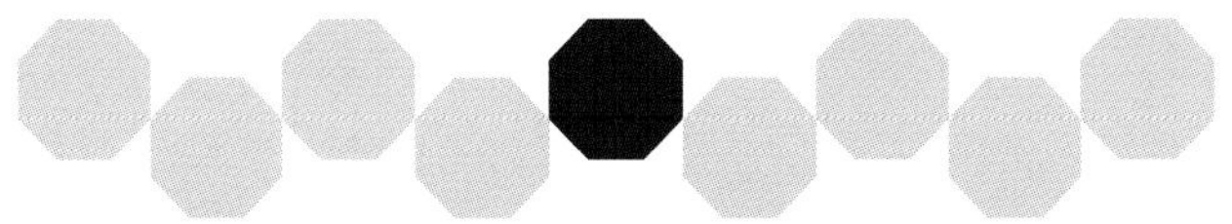

# HOLY WEDNESDAY

# 5

HIEROMONK HERMAN MAJKRZAK

# The Lord's Anointed

*I have found David my servant:*
*with my holy oil have I anointed him.* (Ps 88.20)

*The woman poured precious oil of myrrh upon thine awesome and royal head, O Christ our God.*
— Matins of Holy Wednesday, Ode Eight

## ANOINTING: THE MARK OF KINGSHIP

Among the righteous of the Old Testament, few shine more brightly than King David. God chose him as "a man after his own heart" (1 Sam 13.14), and so much that transpires in Holy Week was foreshadowed in his life.

Our Lord Jesus Christ is David's descendant, and in Christ's kingship are fulfilled all the promises once made to David:

> Thy seed will I establish forever, and set up thy throne from one generation to another… He shall call me: thou art my Father, my God, and the defender of my salvation. And I will make him my first-born, higher than the kings of the earth. (Ps 88.5, 26–27)

King David praying, Greek Book of Hours.

David died, "and his tomb is with us to this day," but these promises were made in prophecy concerning the One who was to come (cf. Acts 2.24–35).

The Anointed: this is everywhere a mark of kingship; it is also the very meaning of the title "Messiah," or "Christ." Whereas David was anointed as king by Samuel the Prophet, the Son of David was anointed not by man, but by the Holy Spirit, who descended upon him in the form of a dove at his baptism in Jordan.

At the midpoint of Holy Week, however, we remember an occasion when Jesus was anointed, not by his "equal in Godhead," as at Theophany, but by his creature, a woman who had "fallen into many sins" (Hymn of Kassiani).

## THE HARLOTRY OF ISRAEL

A repentant harlot: such is the woman we encounter on Holy Wednesday, and in her we perceive a great biblical theme. How often throughout Scripture had God's chosen but unfaithful people been likened to a harlot?

"For long ago you broke your yoke and burst your bonds," we read in Jeremiah, "and you said, 'I will not serve.' Yea, upon every high hill and under every green tree you bowed down as a harlot" (Jer 2.20). And, in Hosea: "My people inquire of a thing of wood, and their staff gives them oracles. A spirit of harlotry has led them astray, and they have left their God to play the harlot" (Hos 4.12).

> The woman poured precious oil of myrrh upon thine awesome and royal head, O Christ our God.

That Israel should have asked for an earthly king at all was an instance of her pining after the ways of the nations. Samuel tried to dissuade them, but to no avail. "No! but we will have a king over us, that we also may be like all the nations, and that our king may govern us and go out before us and fight our battles" (1 Sam 8.19–20).

And so God granted their desire—but not as a sign of favor. Samuel anointed Saul as king, but his reign was bitter, full of turmoil and envy. "Where now is your king, to save you; where are all your princes, to defend you—those of whom you said, 'Give me a king and princes'? I have given you kings in my anger, and I have taken them away in my wrath" (Hos 13.10–11). Indeed, so severe was Saul's reign that, while he still lived, the Lord commanded Samuel to anoint a new king, but in secret: David, the youngest of his own brothers and all but forgotten (1 Sam 16.11–13).

## CHRIST, THE SON OF DAVID

After David's anointing, Saul's spite grew only more intense. For in David, Saul now feared the challenge of a rival, though one who had no need to impose himself or vaunt his divine election. In fact, David fled from Saul in the wilderness where, at one point, he could easily have vanquished Saul forever; yet, Christ-like, he forbore (1 Sam 24.3ff).

"My kingdom," Christ said to Pilate, "is not of this world" (Jn 18.36). In the world men continue to submit themselves to the tyranny of the devil; the prince of this world, like Saul, continues to fill the land with guile and madness, furiously raging against the legitimate authority of God.

After his baptism and the descent of the Spirit, Christ was driven into the wilderness to be challenged and mocked by the evil one. Though it was well within his power at any point to vindicate his rightful claim as Son of God, he, like David, forbore (cf. Mt 4.1–11).

Eventually, all Israel publicly acknowledged David as their ruler. They conceded that it was he who had truly been leading them even while Saul was still alive (cf. 2 Sam 5.1–3).

Christ too was openly recognized by the people: when he entered Jerusalem. They spread their garments before him and shouted "Hosanna to the Son of David!" (Mt 21.9), expecting him to lead them in throwing off the Roman yoke, thus to "restore again the kingdom to Israel" (Acts 1.6). But since Christ's warfare is "not against flesh and blood" (Eph 6.12), the people were disappointed of their hope, and their waning enthusiasm would soon give an opportunity for the Jewish rulers to make their move.

"Even my own familiar friend in whom I trusted, who ate of my bread, has lifted up his heel against me."

David, long into his reign, was betrayed by one of his closest confidants: Ahithophel, whose counsel David trusted as if he had asked at the oracle of God (2 Sam 16.23). With David's son Absalom, Ahithophel conspired against the king, but when his plan came to naught, he despaired and hanged himself (2 Sam 17.23). How bitter is the Psalmist's lament: "Even my own familiar friend in whom I trusted, who ate of my bread, has lifted up his heel against me" (Ps 40.9).

These words hang heavy in the air during the last week of Christ's earthly sojourn as Judas becomes a spy for Christ's enemies (cf. Jn 13.18). Entrusted with the moneybox, the false disciple can barely disguise his greed. Feigning concern for the poor, he begrudges the woman's extravagance as she anoints the Lord with costly oil (cf. Jn 12.4–6). Was Judas, even at that hour, trying to stifle a faint inner misgiving when he saw the woman's torrent of love for the one he had resolved to sell?

> In her heart is gathered all Israel's yearning for communion with God... And like Samuel of old, she anoints in secrecy the true King of the Jews, and on behalf of her people she confesses the Messiah of Israel.

The harlotry of Israel—a millennium and more of lawlessness and idolatry—all this converged as through a funnel upon Iscariot's treacherous heart. Israel always turned aside to other gods, and Judas entrusted himself to the protection of silver. He turned his back on the true God, only to find no hope or refuge in any other. Yet his heart was already so sunk in self-deceit that repentance proved beyond him. Like Ahithophel, despairing, he hanged himself.

## FROM HARLOT TO BRIDE

Yet there is more than this to tell of the fate of Israel. For, alongside Judas, the holy Church also shows us the sinful woman. She too, in her harlotry, is emblematic of faithless Israel. Yet she repents. And in her compunctionate heart is gathered together all Israel's yearning for communion with God: centuries of sacrifices, prayers, and prophetic warnings. The false disciple may betray; the leaders of the Jews may plot and interrogate; Roman soldiers may mock and jeer—but this woman, like Samuel of old, anoints in secrecy the true King of the Jews, and on behalf of her people she confesses the Messiah of Israel.

She anoints the Lord not for the sake of an earthly kingdom, which passes away, but in readiness for death and burial, to which the Lord will submit, that "he might destroy him who has the power of death, that is, the devil, and deliver all those who through fear of death were subject to lifelong slavery" (Heb 2.14–15).

Adam and Eve, like shame-faced slaves, hid from the footsteps of the Lord in paradise. But freed of the guilt of sin through her repentance, this woman draws near to those same beautiful feet with myrrh and tears (cf. Hymn of Kassiani). She is redeemed through Christ and raised to the dignity of a citizen in the New Jerusalem.

As Orthodox Christians we too have been anointed with holy Chrism, that we should be raised even higher than the dignity of citizens: that we should reign with Christ forever (cf. Rev 22.5). Our anointing, like Christ's, is a preparation for burial. Before we can reign with him, we must suffer with him and not deny him (1 Tim 2.12); only through being buried with him can we be raised up to newness of life (cf. Rom 6.4, 8). Vladimir Lossky puts it thus:

The sinful woman anoints Christ's feet, detail, English Psalter.

> We have received the royal unction of the Holy Spirit, but we do not yet reign with Christ. Like the young David, who after his anointing by Samuel had to endure Saul's hatred before he obtained his kingdom, we must resist the armies of Satan, who like Saul is dispossessed but still remains "the prince of this world." [1]

The treacherous disciple grew faint at the sight of battle and gave himself over to evil and eternal death. But the woman, through repentance, put on the armor of salvation, fought the good fight, and took hold of eternal life (1 Tim 6.12).

❀ ❀ ❀

Through such warfare, a sin-loving harlot is transformed into a pure bride, adorned for her husband. Throughout the long, moonless night of this age, she keeps watch with joy for the midnight coming of the divine Bridegroom. Wise in her renewed virginity, she keeps her lamp full of oil and burning brightly. She is ready, when he comes, to be led by him into the eternal Bridal Chamber, there to partake of his delights.

# ABOUT THE AUTHOR

**Hieromonk Herman Majkrzak**, a monk at St Tikhon's Monastery, South Canaan, Pennsylvania, is a graduate of Westminster Choir College, Princeton, New Jersey, and of St Tikhon's Seminary. He taught liturgical music and liturgical theology at St Herman's Seminary, Kodiak, Alaska, from 2005 to 2007, and was the choir director and music instructor at St Vladimir's Seminary from 2010 to 2016.

IC XC
Θ
Φ

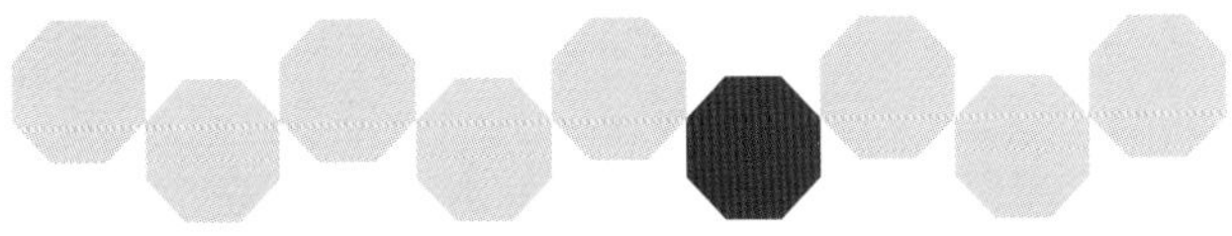

# HOLY THURSDAY

6

PROFESSOR PAUL MEYENDORFF

# A Meditation

*Great art thou, O Lord, and marvelous are thy works, and there is no word which suffices to hymn thy wonders!*

## A REJECTED MESSIAH

These words, which come from the blessing of water at the baptismal service and at the water blessing on Theophany, are probably not the first words that come to mind now, at the midpoint of Holy Week.[1] This is hardly a time for celebration.

We are now at the point in Holy Week when things go from bad to worse. The shouts of "Hosanna" have long faded, and the crowds will soon be yelling, "Crucify him! Crucify him!"

The religious authorities, threatened by Jesus' popularity and by his assaults on their traditions, are plotting to kill him. The civil

This is hardly a time for celebration. We are now at the point in Holy Week when things go from bad to worse.

authorities have their own agendas, focused on maintaining their positions of power and preserving the *pax Romana*. Judas, one of the Twelve, is laying his own plans to betray the Master, even as he eats and drinks at the Last Supper with the Lord and the other disciples. And immediately after the supper, the disciples begin to argue among themselves about which of them is the greatest.

Soon, the disciples will abandon him as he undergoes the Passion. Peter will deny him three times, and all the apostles will scatter after Jesus' arrest. Only a few women remain faithful as they accompany him at his Crucifixion and later as they come to anoint his dead body—and for this reason they become the first witnesses to the Resurrection.

No one knows or comprehends the cosmic events that are taking place. The world at large is completely oblivious, and the story of Jesus leaves almost no mark in the official historical records of the day. The Jewish nation rejects the Messiah as, at best, another prophet who met a sad end—he was certainly not the triumphant, worldly king they were expecting. Jesus' followers, bewildered and confused, give up. Even the women who remain faithful do so not because they understand the significance of what is happening, but because of the personal love they feel for him.

## A REJECTING PEOPLE

And what about us, who gather together some two thousand years later to remember these events? As the texts of the Holy Week services make abundantly clear, we are just like those weak, sinful individuals portrayed in the scripture readings and in the hymnography. Indeed, it is to us that these texts are addressed. We are just like those crowds that yell "Hosanna" one day, and a few days later crucify our Lord. We do this whenever we despise or ignore our neighbor, who is the living image of Christ. We do this when, like the Pharisees, we concern ourselves more with the externals of the faith than with the law of love. We do this when, like Judas, we value the thirty pieces of silver more than the gift of eternal life.

The Holy Week liturgical cycle functions as one big parable: a story that first draws us in, and then pulls the rug out from under us as it reveals the weakness of all our own arguments, our own rationalizations. We think that it is the Jews who are responsible for crucifying Christ—and at one time people calling themselves Orthodox Christians would launch pogroms against Jews on these days. We may even consider that some of the Holy Thursday and Holy Friday texts are anti-Semitic, and we fail to realize that they are actually speaking about us. For it is by our own sins and actions that we crucify Christ. It is we who stand condemned.

Judas leads the multitude, T'oros Roslin Gospels.

These Holy Week services thus paint a dark picture of the fallen world in which we live. This is a world in which darkness reigns, where individuals and nations commit the vilest atrocities and genocides. Modernity, despite bringing much improvement to the lives of so many people, has also made the extermination of entire peoples ever more efficient and impersonal. Our cities are full of

Parable of the Banquet, Nikola Sarić.

suffering and crime, and that, in the richest nation on this earth. And in many parts of the world, conditions are far worse.

In short, these services unmask the reality of this world, a reality we try so hard to conceal even from ourselves. Like the emperor in the familiar fairy tale, we are revealed as having no clothes. Or, in the language of the *exaposteilarion* that we sing at the Matins services from Monday to Thursday of this week, we have no "wedding garment" to enter into the bridal chamber.

These services unmask the reality of this world, a reality we try so hard to conceal even from ourselves. Like the emperor in the fairy tale, we are revealed as having no clothes.

## A REDEEMING SAVIOR

Yet it is only when we become aware of this absolute emptiness that we can begin to understand why it was necessary for Christ to come into the world in order to overcome this darkness. We begin to see this now, as Christ first washes the feet of his disciples, then offers his Body and Blood to us, in anticipation of his own death on the Cross for our sake. He, and he alone, is under no delusion. He alone sees this fallen world for what it is—a world that rejects its Maker.

> The One who created the world never stops loving his creation, even when that creation does not return his love.

And yet, as we hear in John's Gospel, God so loved the world that he sent his only-begotten Son, who, by his presence among us, fills the darkness with light. The One who created the world never stops loving his creation, even when that creation does not return his love and chases after idols.

Later today, as we celebrate the eucharistic liturgy of Holy Thursday, we shall sing "One is holy, one is the Lord, Jesus Christ." As we do this, we confess not only that he alone is holy, but also that we, because of our sins, are not. Yet we do this with the certainty that through him we too become holy, not because of anything that we do or have done but because he freely bestows his holiness on us. We become holy when, at our baptism and chrismation, we are clothed with the "robe of righteousness." And we reaffirm this each time we approach the chalice.

The garment that we lack is provided to us freely by the Master. At the time of Christ, the host would provide a wedding garment to all the guests he invited. They did not have to purchase or earn it for themselves. So, in the familiar parable about the wedding feast, the man who comes without the proper attire does so only because he has rejected the free gift of the garment from the Master (Mt 22.11–13).

Our calling today, as we prepare for the Liturgy of Holy Thursday, is not to reject that gift, that festal, baptismal garment, but to accept it with gratitude, knowing full well that we do not deserve it. It is for this that Christ comes to us, and why he accepts to suffer and to die on our behalf. This, even more than the many miracles that Jesus performed during his sojourn among us, is the greatest wonder of all.

> *Great art thou, O Lord, and marvelous are thy works, and there is no word which suffices to hymn thy wonders!*

## ABOUT THE AUTHOR

**Paul Meyendorff** was the Father Alexander Schmemann Professor of Liturgical Theology. His own writings include *The Service of the Anointing of the Sick* and *Russia, Ritual, and Reform* (St Vladimir's Seminary Press). He also is Series Editor for the Orthodox Liturgy series published by the seminary press, and Editor of *St Vladimir's Theological Quarterly*.

7

PROTOPRESBYTER
ALEXANDER SCHMEMANN

# The Last Supper

Two events shape the Liturgy of Great and Holy Thursday: the Last Supper of Christ with his disciples, and the betrayal by Judas. The meaning of both is found in *love*.

The Last Supper is the ultimate revelation of God's redeeming love for man, of love as the very essence of salvation. And the betrayal of Judas reveals that sin, death, and self-destruction are also due to love, but to deviated and distorted love, love directed at that which does not deserve love. Here is the mystery of this unique day (and its liturgy, where light and darkness, joy and sorrow, are so strange-

> Two events shape the Liturgy of Great and Holy Thursday: the Last Supper of Christ with his disciples, and the betrayal by Judas. The meaning of both is found in *love.*

ly mixed), which challenges us with the choice on which depends the eternal destiny of each one of us.

## DIVINE LOVE IN CREATION

"Now before the feast of the Passover, when Jesus knew that his hour was come… having loved his own which were in the world, he loved them unto the end…" (Jn 13.1). To understand the meaning of the Last Supper we must see it as the very end of the great movement of Divine Love, which began with the creation of the world and is now to be consummated in the death and Resurrection of Christ.

God is Love (1 Jn 4.8). And the first gift of Love was life. The meaning, the content of life was *communion*. To be alive, a human being was to eat and to drink, to partake of the world. The world was thus Divine Love made food, and food made body of Adam. And being alive, that is, partaking of the world, "Adam" (the human being) was to be in communion with God, to have God as the meaning, the content, and the end-all of life. Communion with the God-given world was indeed communion with God.

Adam received food from God, and making it his body and his life, he offered the whole world back to God; he transformed it into life in God and with God. The love of God gave life to man, and the love of Adam for God transformed this life into communion with God. This was paradise. And, life in it was, indeed, *eucharistic.*[1] Through Adam and his love for God, the whole creation was to be sanctified and transformed into one all-embracing sacrament of Divine Presence, and Adam was the priest of this sacrament.

Adam and Eve in paradise, Armenian hymnal.

But in sin man lost this eucharistic life. He lost it because he ceased to see the world as means of communion with God and his life as eucharistic, that is, as adoration and thanksgiving. He loved himself and the world for their own sake; he made himself the content and the end-all of his life. He thought that his hunger and thirst, that is, the dependence of his life on the world—could be satisfied by the world as such, by food as such.

But world and food, once they are deprived of their initial sacramental meaning (as means of communion with God); once they are not received for God's sake, and filled with hunger and thirst for God; once, in other words, God is no longer their real "content," can give no life, can satisfy no hunger—for they have no life in themselves. And thus by putting his love in them, man deviated his love from the only object of all love, of all hunger, of all desires. *And he died*. For death is the inescapable "decomposition" of life cut from its only source and content.

The Last Supper, fresco, Cyprus.

Man thought to find life in the world and in food, but he found death. His life became communion with death, for instead of transforming the world—by faith, love, and adoration—into communion with God, he submitted himself entirely to the world; he ceased to be its priest and became its slave. And by his sin the whole world was made a cemetery, where people condemned to death partook of death and "sat in the region and shadow of death" (Mt 4.16).

But though Adam betrayed, God remained faithful. He did not "turn himself away forever from his creature whom he had made, neither did he forget the works of his hands, but he visited him in diverse manners, through the tender compassion of his mercy."[2]

## DIVINE LOVE IN RE-CREATION

A new divine work began, that of redemption and salvation. And it was fulfilled in Christ, the Son of God, who, in order to restore Adam to his pristine beauty and to restore life as communion with God, became human, and took upon himself our nature with its thirst and hunger, with its desire for and love of life.

And in him, life was revealed, given, accepted, and fulfilled as total and perfect "Eucharist," as total and perfect communion with God. He rejected the basic human temptation to live "by bread alone"; rather, he revealed that God and his kingdom are the real food, the real life of man. And this perfect eucharistic life, filled with God—and, therefore divine and immortal—he gave to all those who would believe in him, that is, who would find in him the meaning and the content of their lives.

Such is the wonderful meaning of the Last Supper.

Such is the wonderful meaning of the Last Supper. He offered himself as the true food of man, because the life revealed in him is true Life. And thus, the movement of divine Love that began in paradise with an offer to "take, eat..." (for eating is life for man) comes now "at the end" with the offer to "take, eat, this is my Body..."(for God is the Life of all mankind). The Last Supper is the restoration of the *paradise of bliss*, of life as Eucharist and Communion.

But this hour of ultimate love is also that of ultimate betrayal. Judas leaves the light of the Upper Room and goes into darkness: "And it was night," states the Gospel (Jn 13.30).

> Money stands here for all deviated and distorted love that leads a human being into betraying God—indeed, it stands for all love that has been *stolen* from God, and Judas, therefore, is the *Thief*.

Why does he leave? Because he loves, answers the Gospel, and his fateful love is stressed again and again in the hymns of Holy Thursday. It does not matter indeed, that he loves the "silver." Money stands here for all deviated and distorted love that leads a person into betraying God—indeed, it stands for all love that has been *stolen* from God, and Judas, therefore, is the *Thief*.

Judas betrays Jesus with a kiss, detail, Danish Psalter.

When we human beings (Adam and Eve) do not love God and in God, we still love and desire—for we were created to love, and love is our nature—but it becomes then a dark and self-destroying passion, and death waits at its end. And each year, as we immerse ourselves into the unfathomable light and depth of Holy Thursday, the same decisive question is addressed to each one of us: "Do I respond to Christ's love and accept it as my life, or do I follow Judas into the darkness of his night?"

The Liturgy of Holy Thursday includes Matins, Vespers, and (following Vespers) the Liturgy of St Basil the Great. In the cathedral churches the special service of the "Washing of the Feet" takes place after the Liturgy. The deacon reads the Gospel, and the bishop washes the feet of twelve priests, reminding us that Christ's love is

At Matins, the Troparion sets the theme of the day: the opposition between the love of Christ and the "insatiable desire" of Judas.

the foundation of life in the Church, and it shapes all relations within it. Also on Holy Thursday, the primates of autocephalous Churches consecrate holy chrism, which signifies that the new love of Christ is the gift we receive from the Holy Spirit on the day of our entrance into the Church.

At Matins, the Troparion sets the theme of the day: the opposition between the love of Christ and the "insatiable desire" of Judas.

*When the glorious disciples were illumined by washing at the Supper, then was the impious Judas darkened with the love of silver, and to the unjust judges does he betray thee, the just Judge. Consider, O lover of money, him who hanged himself because of it. Do not follow the insatiable desire that dared this against the Master. O Lord, good to all, glory to thee.*

After the Gospel reading (Lk 12.1–40), we are given a contemplation regarding the mystical and eternal meaning of the Last Supper, found within the beautiful *Canon of St Cosmas*. Its last *Irmos* (9th Ode) invites us to share in the hospitality of the Lord's banquet:

> *Come, O ye faithful, let us enjoy the hospitality of the Lord and the banquet of immortality, in the upper chamber with minds uplifted...*

At Vespers, the *stichera* (i.e., hymns) set for the Psalm "Lord, I have cried" stress the spiritual anticlimax of Holy Thursday, the betrayal of Judas:

> *Judas the slave and knave, the disciple and traitor, the friend and fiend, was proved by his deeds. For, as he followed the Master, within himself he contemplated his betrayal…*

The Last Supper, detail.

After the entrance are three lessons from the Old Testament:

1. Exodus 19.10–19: God's descent from Mount Sinai to his people, as the image of God's coming in the Eucharist;

2. Job 38.1–23, 42.1–5: God's conversation with Job, and Job's answer, "…who will utter to me what I understand not? Things too great and wonderful for me, which I knew not…" These "great and wonderful things" are fulfilled in the gift of Christ's Body and Blood; and

3. Isaiah 50.4–11: the beginning of the prophecies about the Suffering Servant of God.

From the light of Holy Thursday we enter in to the darkness of Holy Friday, the day of Christ's Passion, death, and burial.

The Epistle reading is from 1 Corinthians 11.23–32: St Paul's account of the Last Supper and the meaning of Communion.

The Gospel reading (the longest of the year) is taken from all four Gospels and is the full story of the Last Supper, the betrayal of Judas, and Christ's arrest in the garden.

The Cherubic Hymn and the Hymn of Communion are replaced by the words of the usual prayer before Holy Communion:

> *Of thy Mystical Supper, O Son of God, accept me today as a communicant. For I will not speak of thy mysteries to thine enemies; neither like Judas will I give thee a kiss, but like the thief will I confess thee, remember me, O Lord, in thy kingdom.*

From the light of Holy Thursday we enter in to the darkness of Holy Friday, the day of Christ's Passion, death, and burial. In the early Church this day was called "Pascha of the Cross," for it is indeed the beginning of that Passover, or *Passage*, whose whole meaning will be gradually revealed to us: first, in the wonderful quiet of the Great and Blessed Sabbath, and, then, in the joy of the day of Resurrection.

## ABOUT THE AUTHOR

**Protopresbyter Alexander Schmemann** (+1983) served as Dean of St Vladimir's Seminary for more than two decades. A prolific writer, his deep and visionary reflections upon the liturgical services of the Orthodox Christian Church influenced thousands around the globe. His books *Great Lent* and *Holy Week* (St Vladimir's Seminary Press)—the latter being the volume from which this essay was taken—both contain exceptional meditations on the liturgical services of the Lenten season.

# 8

PROTOPRESBYTER THOMAS HOPKO

# Remember Me, O Lord

The Lord God has graced us once again. He has counted us worthy, by his great mercy, that we should be gathered for this Divine Liturgy. God has blessed us and allowed us to celebrate the mystical supper on the day of the mystical supper, the supper that he commanded would be done in remembrance of him until he comes again in glory, the supper when Christ ate the Passover meal with his apostles before his passion.

He said, "Do this in remembrance of me" (Lk 22.19). We are blessed today to keep that commandment and to do this in remembrance of him. What we need to remember, what we need to do, what we need to say, what we need to hear, and what we need to believe and confess are given to us by God in this magnificent Divine Liturgy of St Basil the Great.

## THE GIFT OF PARADISE

In this Divine Liturgy, we will remember and proclaim the entire plan of God—all of the marvelous, wonderful works of God for the sake of our salvation. We will remember and proclaim that we have been created by God and honored with his own image. He created us to be, as the anaphora prayer says, in a "paradise of delight" that promises eternal life and the enjoyment of everlasting blessings.

The Last Supper, Psalter illustration, French.

So we remember, we proclaim, and we celebrate that we have been given the honor of living in paradise, enjoying God's blessings forever. These blessings are nothing less than the very qualities of God himself. Our delight—and our paradise—is to live within the communion of the Holy Trinity of the uncreated Godhead, the Father and the Son and the Holy Spirit, and to enjoy these unending blessings by keeping his commandments.

Christ himself also said in his last discourse with his disciples, "If you love me, you will keep my commandments" (Jn 14.15). In the First Letter of John, it says that if we love God and know the love of God, then we will keep his commandments. His commandments are not burdensome; they are blessed commandments that lead us to life in paradise, to communion with God (1 Jn 5.2–3).

We know that we don't keep his commandments. Human beings, wherever they are, have not kept his commandments. Therefore, we've lost paradise.

## THE LOSS OF PARADISE

However, we know that we don't keep his commandments. Human beings wherever they are have not kept his commandments. Therefore, we've lost paradise; we don't have the enjoyment of God's blessings.

But, we also confess and proclaim that God so loved the world that he sent his own Son to keep the commandments (Jn 3.16). Christ the Messiah, Jesus born of the Virgin, came on the earth to keep the commandments so that we might have paradise. Jesus alone, the New Adam, loved God totally—the God who is love, his Father—with all his mind, with all his soul, with all his heart, and with all his strength. Jesus alone loved his neighbor—his brothers and sisters, and even his worst enemies—as he loved his very self.

Jesus found himself loving those enemies... and we are all his enemies. We are all the ones who crucified him. We can't blame anybody else. Each one of us, personally and individually, is guilty of the crucifixion of Christ because we do not keep the commandments.

Our holy Fathers even claim that we Christians, in that sense, are worse than other people (and Orthodox Christians are worse than *all* other people), because we know the truth: we believe it; we confess it; and we pray it every Sunday. Still we sin and still we break those commandments, and therefore we break our communion with God. We turn paradise into hell.

But as it says in the baptismal service that every one of us has experienced, the Lord could not stand to see the world oppressed by the devil, so he came and he saved us by keeping the commandments for us. He saved us by giving us the power, through his victory over death, to keep the commandments with him.

A unique feature of today's liturgy is the entrance hymn:

> *Of thy Mystical Supper, O Son of God,*
> *accept me today as a communicant.*
> *For I will not speak of thy mysteries to thine enemies;*
> *neither like Judas will I give thee a kiss,*
> *but like the thief will I confess thee:*
> *Remember me, O Lord, in thy kingdom.*

Today, when we bring the bread and the wine in remembrance of Christ and place it on the altar; when we lift it up to God and remember all the saving actions of God and the ultimate saving action ("This is my body broken. This is my blood shed for the life of the world, for the remission of sins."); when we participate in Holy Communion and experience the paradise of delight, we sing this same hymn.

We crucified him. We can't blame anybody else. Each one of us, personally and individually, is guilty of the crucifixion of Christ because we do not keep the commandments.

Then, after Holy Communion is over, in place of the normal song of thanksgiving, "Let our mouths be filled with Thy praise, O Lord," we sing this same song again. The *Typikon* even says that while we receive Holy Communion, we are just to sing this same song again, and again, and again.

Unlike all the other prayers and hymns of the Divine Liturgy (except for the Creed, by which we reaffirm our baptism, and the prayer before Holy Communion where we say, "I believe, O Lord, and I confess..."), today's entrance hymn is sung in the singular. We don't sing: "Of your mystical supper, O Son of God, accept us today as communicants; for we will not speak of your mystery to your enemies, we will not give you a kiss like Judas." It doesn't say "we." It says "me," and it says "I."

This is because each one of us has to say this personally. *There is no "communion" except for the communion of persons in communion.* And there's only communion if each person can say for herself, for himself: "I believe in one God, the Father Almighty. I believe in one Lord Jesus Christ. I believe in the Holy Spirit, the Lord and the Giver of Life. I believe in one Holy Catholic and Apostolic Church" and "I believe, O Lord, and I confess that you are truly the Christ, the Son of the living God, who came into the world to save sinners, of whom I am first."

I am the first among sinners—not someone else, not some Adam and Eve a long time ago, not some bad people somewhere else, not all the other godless or faithless people out there. No. "Of thy Mystical Supper, O Son of God, accept me today as a communicant. For I will not speak of thy mysteries to thine enemies; neither like Judas will I give thee a kiss, but like the thief will I confess thee: Remember me, O Lord, in Thy kingdom."

> We will say it again and again: "I will not give you a kiss like Judas."

This hymn is not a prayer. It doesn't say, "O Lord, please don't let me give you a kiss like Judas. O Lord, please remember me." We don't say that. We say, "I will not give thee a kiss like Judas," and every time that we sin, we should remember that we have said this. In this Divine Liturgy, we will say it again and again: "I will not give

Judas betrays Jesus, Danish Psalter.

thee a kiss like Judas. I will not speak of thy mysteries to thine enemies. I will confess thee. Remember me, O Lord, in thy kingdom." If we dare to say this, we should never forget, for one second of our lives, that this is what we said.

This personal statement is just like the one we said on the day of our baptism. The priest asked us (or, our sponsor), "Dost thou believe in Christ?" and we responded, "Yes, I believe in Christ." And he asked again, "Dost thou believe in him as thy Lord and King?"

and we reaffirmed our faith by saying, "I believe in him as Lord and King. I believe in one God the Father Almighty…." Our faith has to be personal. We need one another, but each one of us has to believe for ourselves.

## "TODAY, THOU WILT BE WITH ME IN PARADISE"

In the Epistle reading for today, St Paul says, "Let us participate in a worthy manner" (1 Cor 11.23–32). Being "worthy" doesn't amount to saying certain prayers and not eating meat. That doesn't make us worthy. The only thing that makes us worthy is discerning the Lord's Body, confessing that we're not worthy. No one is worthy. We are all sinners: "There's no one righteous, no not one" (Rom 3:10). The condition for participating in the mystical supper is to confess and say, "Lord, I am not worthy. You make me worthy. I am not deserving, but it is because of your broken Body and your spilled Blood that I can participate."

Christ and the Good Thief, Titian.

We can accept the invitation to enjoy the Master's hospitality in the upper room with uplifted minds, and not only that, but we can also already enjoy the paradise of the age to come, given to us in the Church! The condition is to discern the Lord's Body, to know that we're sinners. If we know that we are sinners, then we don't judge anybody for anything. We don't look at what other people are doing. We just look at ourselves. When we discern the Lord's Body, we can say to God, "Remember me. Jesus, remember me when thou comest into thy kingdom." And then we will hear those incredible words: "Today, you will be with me in paradise" (Lk 23.43).

Christ is in his kingdom, and the kingdom is here. And he says to us, today, right now, "You will be with me in paradise."

As a matter of fact, today we *are* with him in paradise. Today, we are with Jesus in paradise as long as we know that we're sinners. Even though we may give Jesus a kiss of betrayal, let us not be given over to despair like Judas was. But, every time that we give Jesus such a kiss, we must remember that we said, "I will not give thee a kiss as did Judas, but like the thief will I confess thee."

That thief was a miserable sinner, just like the fallen woman we heard about on Holy Wednesday, but when we identify with both of them, when we see ourselves as sinners, then our whole life becomes paradise.

"Remember me, O Lord, when thou comest into thy kingdom." Christ is in his kingdom, and the kingdom is here. And he says to us, today, right now, "Thou wilt be with me in paradise."

## ABOUT THE AUTHOR

**Protopresbyter Thomas Hopko** (+2015) was Dean of St Vladimir's Orthodox Theological Seminary from 1992 until his retirement in 2002 as Dean Emeritus. He also taught classes in Dogmatic Theology, Practical Theology, Homiletics, and Spirituality at the Seminary, and authored several books, including *The Orthodox Faith* series, and *The Winter Pascha* (SVS Press, 1984).

# 9

ARCHPRIEST ALEXANDER RENTEL

# A Feast of Humility

Every year, the services of Holy Week bring before us selections from the Old Testament: of Jacob, of Joseph and his brothers, and of the great prophets Moses and Job. We also hear the ancient prophecies of Isaiah and Jeremiah, which make us aware that everything that has happened before, everything that has been spoken in Scripture, reaches its fulfillment in our Lord's Passion. The Gospel passages read during this solemn week also recount Christ's final teachings to his disciples, and the events that lead to his Passion.

> The services speak of an "end" to Jesus' sojourn on earth, but now, as Holy Week draws to a conclusion, they also speak of a "beginning."

As the services progress, the pace of the drama of Christ's last week on earth quickens, as our Savior hastens to the events that are so familiar to us: the supper, the trial, the scourging, the haggard procession with the Cross, and the brutal Crucifixion itself. The church services speak of an "end" to Jesus' sojourn on earth, but now, as Holy Week draws to a conclusion, they also speak of a "beginning." They inform us about what is old and approaching the darkness of death, and about what is new and emerging into the light of life.

## THE NATURAL WORLD AND CREATION

Even all around us outside, the natural world is beginning to proclaim this pattern of life and light: the sun casts more light upon the earth, dispersing the night's darkness. And the season reminds us of King Solomon's poetic words, "For lo, the winter is past, the rain is over and gone. The flowers appear on the earth, the time of singing has come" (Song 2.11–12).

Interestingly, the Hebrews also had reckoned the date of their annual commemoration of Pascha (i.e., Passover) according to this natural order: "In the first month, on the fourteenth day of the month in the evening, is the Lord's Pascha" (Lev 23.5–6). Commenting on the "Lord's Pascha," some Church Fathers seized on its theme of annual re-creation and used images from the Passover to describe the liturgical season of the death and Resurrection of Christ. Many Fathers even noted that spring was traditionally thought to be the season of the creation of the world; so, it became natural for Christians to view Holy Week and our Lord's death and Resurrection as a recapitulation of the original creation.

Peach Blossoms, John William Hill.

This "new creation," in our liturgical cycle, begins on Lazarus Saturday, continuing through Palm Sunday, when our Lord once again separates light from darkness, as he calls forth his dead friend to life. As the great King and true Light of the world, meekly bearing salvation, he enters into his city, Jerusalem, to great acclamation. The coming of his light increases even more as his death, burial, and Resurrection draw near. Finally, in the face of the brilliant light of our Lord's Passion, as he hangs on the Cross, the two lights of the natural creation, the sun and the moon, diminish and no longer illumine the world.

On this holiest of all Fridays, our God fashions the human being anew, just as his Christ is being crucified. From the side of the "New Adam" comes not a rib, but rather, blood and water, through which he establishes and nourishes the Church. After this comes the Great and Holy Sabbath, the last day of the old creation, the Saturday on which God will rest once again. And on the next day, the eighth day, the first day of the new creation, the human being—of the earth and once bound by death—will be freed by life in Christ Jesus. There will be a new creation, peopled by those who have been formed by his word, nourished on the food of his body, and illumined by the light of his power.

## THE FIFTH DAY OF CREATION, AND RE-CREATION IN THE FOOT WASHING

On this fifth day of Holy Week, on this Holy Thursday, our attention is drawn to numerous themes—the Mystical Supper, the scheming of the elders, the treachery of Judas. But let us stop and consider only one event of this day, the washing of the feet of Jesus' disciples. On Holy Thursday, the waters splash as they did on the original fifth day, not with every sort of sea creature, but with our Savior calling forth a new way of life for his new creation.

With the knowledge "that the Father had given all things into his hands" (Jn 13.3), the eternal Word of God stoops down and humbly puts his hands in the basin of water to wash his disciples' feet. By

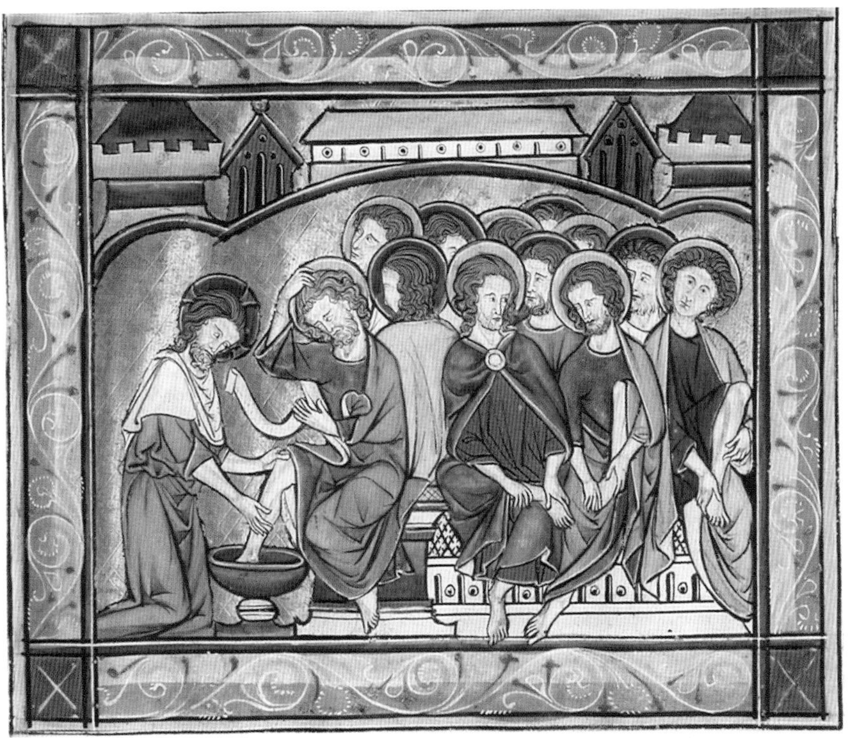

Jesus washes the disciples' feet, Psalter illustration, French.

this humble act, as he washes away the filth and grime from feet that trod upon the dusty paths of Palestine and through the alleys of Jerusalem, he will create new winged creatures; the "new Adam" will soar to the heavenly heights of virtue and will keep company with the angels in the presence of God the Father, with his Son, in the Holy Spirit.

The hymnography of Holy Thursday speaks of the washing of the feet as the time "when the disciples were illumined." Illumination is, of course, also the way the Church speaks of the mystery of Holy Baptism. The Church can use this term for both the washing of the feet and Holy Baptism, because the results are the same: we put on Christ, who is our Teacher and Lord, and strive to be all that he is, by doing what he has commanded.

Jesus says as much plainly: "If I then, your Lord and Teacher, have washed your feet, you also ought to wash one another's feet. For I have given you an example, that you also should do as I have done to you" (Jn 13.14–15). This is how the heavenly heights are opened for us: we will ascend to the heavens when we understand what Jesus did to his disciples and for us, and when, further, we follow his command to "wash one another's feet."

Christ washes the disciples' feet, Armenian hymnal.

We should make no mistake: "foot washing" is not an easy task even now, in our world with all the benefits of modern hygiene! The extent of our Lord's love for us can be seen precisely in this, as he takes the filthy, dirty feet of his disciples and washes them clean. The dirt and grime are precisely what makes this act so beautiful. In that soiled water, our Lord has called forth new life, a life purified and clean. He has called forth life that proclaims power in weakness, the triumph of humility and service, the victory of love, and the death of selfishness.

Out of these waters, just like the waters of baptism, he has not called us to be proud or powerful. He has not empowered us to be self-centered or self-interested. He has not challenged us to become successful men or women by the standards of the world. No, he has called us to emulate him: if we have called him our Lord and King at our baptism, we ought to "wash one another's feet," just as our Lord and Teacher has done.

On this fifth day of Holy Week, we are given a vision of God's new creation. For all of us who live within this new creation, "washing one another's feet" means giving ourselves to one another in all love, humility, and service. The new creation is to be populated by those who are willing to beautifully

The dirt and grime are precisely what makes this act so beautiful. In that soiled water, our Lord has called forth new life… life that proclaims power in weakness, the triumph of humility, the victory of love, and the death of selfishness.

debase themselves and wash the feet of their brothers and sisters; to offer themselves, to humble themselves, to give entirely of themselves, not being concerned by position, status, authority, pride, pomp, or any consideration other than loving their brother and sister the way the Lord has loved them, and in exactly the same fashion.

Fathers, brothers, and sisters, as we stand ready to ascend to the "upper chamber" (as the church service beckons), and, as companions of our Lord, to partake of the Divine Word, let us commit ourselves once more to Jesus Christ, who is going to his voluntary passion for us and for our salvation, to inaugurate a new creation. Let us pray that by emulating our Lord in our words, deeds, and thoughts, we may find ourselves in that chamber with him, and with all those who have been well pleasing to him from all the ages. Amen.

## ABOUT THE AUTHOR

**Archpriest Alexander Rentel** is Assistant Professor of Canon Law and Byzantine Studies, and The John and Paraskeva Skvir Lecturer in Practical Theology at St Vladimir's Seminary.

KÖNIG DER
HERRLICHKEIT
IC XC

# HOLY FRIDAY

10

ARCHPRIEST EUGEN J. PENTIUC

# A Crucifying Silence: A Messianic Reading of Psalm 22

> *About the ninth hour Jesus cried with a loud voice, saying, "Eli, Eli, lama sabachthani?" that is to say, "My God, my God, why hast thou forsaken me?"* (Mt 27.46, cf. Mk 15.34)
>
> *"My God, my God, why hast thou forsaken me? How far from my salvation, the words of my roaring!"* (Ps 22.1–2)

## YEAR AD 33, APRIL 3, FRIDAY

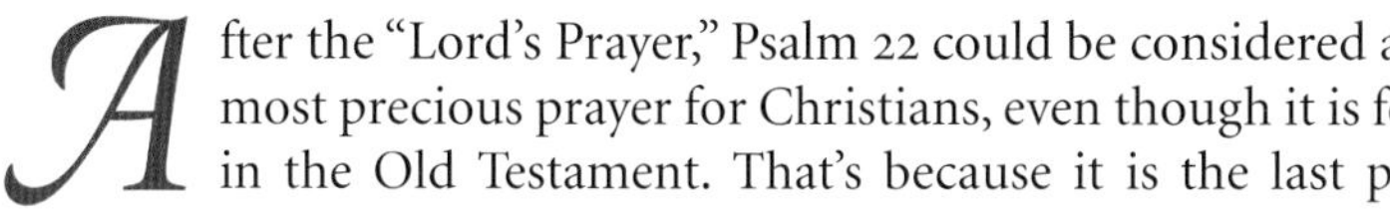

After the "Lord's Prayer," Psalm 22 could be considered as the most precious prayer for Christians, even though it is found in the Old Testament. That's because it is the last prayer

# My God, my God, why have you forsaken me?

uttered by our Lord Jesus Christ, the suffering and dying Messiah.

Having been, during his last days on earth, "exceedingly sorrowful, even unto death" (Mt 26.38), the crucified Jesus begins praying Psalm 22. However, he prays not in Hebrew—the language of scribes and priests—but in Aramaic, his mother's tongue, as one can notice from the Greek spelling of the Aramaic translation (*targum*) of Psalm 22, as recorded in the Gospel according to St Matthew.

When studied within its initial biblical context and in its original language, this messianic psalm can help us understand our Lord's perplexing words on the Cross and deepen our comprehension of salvation. Indeed, comparing the experience of the original psalmist, King David, with that of the Messiah, our Lord Jesus Christ (who repeats his words at the Crucifixion), can help us apprehend how this prophetic psalm is fulfilled on the Cross.

For example, in verses 14–16 of Psalm 22, the reference to a "a pack of evildoers" symbolizes either humans and/or demons, who were "encircling" the psalmist, pushing in on him, eager to see the outcome of the awesome, unpredictable confrontation between light and darkness; eager to see if the sufferer would be able to overcome this last temptation. The psalmist's suffering in Psalm 22 is amplified by his perception of having been abandoned by God. The psalmist already has been accused by violent, fanatic witnesses. He has been condemned by enemies, forsaken by friends, and ridiculed by bystanders—both commoners and the ruling class. Even in the face of such malevolence, however, the psalmist trusts in the God of his fathers, and in the final analysis, his trust does not waver.

At his moment of suffering, however, questions occur: Has he the strength to resist the last and greatest test of all? Is he truly abandoned by the very same God whom he has served passionately, even reluctantly? Will he become another "Job" by evading the act of cursing God, thus depriving himself of one last exploit of freedom and human pleasure: the "art" of cursing another, of blaming one's ill fortune on anyone other than oneself?

## DESPAIR, PRAISE, AND A ROAR OF VICTORY

Those who read Psalm 22.1–2 and its New Testament parallels are often puzzled by the despairing tone of the Messiah's question, "My God, my God, why hast thou forsaken me?" At first sight, his words may resemble a child's repeated yet hopeless plea, like an entreaty whimpered just prior to his bursting into tears and running to hide in his room. A careful examination of the context, however, reveals that the question in Psalm 22.1–2 is a cry of genuine distress rather than of hopelessness or despair—as was King David's.

A careful examination reveals that Christ's question is a cry of genuine distress rather than of hopelessness or despair—as was King David's.

Psalm 22 may be divided into two clear sections: the first 21 verses express feelings of desertion and humiliation, and recall threats of death (with all the accompanying emotional distress), while verses 22–31 contain praise and commitment to Yahweh, as well as a universal recognition of Yahweh's victory and dominion on earth and in heaven. An old and pious Christian tradition recounts that Jesus, while hanging on the Cross, began his recitation of prayer with Psalm 22.1–2 and then continued through the following psalms, and lastly gave up his Spirit when he came to Psalm 31.5, "Into thy hand I commit my Spirit, thou hast redeemed me, Yahweh, faithful God" (cf. Lk 23.46). So, in the final analysis, both our Lord Jesus and King David were "victorious" because they had placed their hope in God.

King David kneeling in penitence, Grisaille Book of Hours.

Moreover, it is critical to realize in the messianic reading of the Psalms that Jesus experienced the full array of human emotion; he was not merely stoic in the face of his own death. He lived and died as a member of humanity, but expressed his true divinity and relationship to the eternal Father at the end of his humble life.

While agonizing in his last moments on Cross, he experienced just what any one of us might experience, from a moment of despair and seeming solitude, to trust and joy that led him to praise Yahweh. The fullness and depth of his humanity, as revealed in his experience of the Cross, ought to serve as an example to us, leading us all to the same humility and perseverance. Just like the psalmist, Jesus, the Messiah, did not die in solitude, abandoned by God, but rather he went to his death awash in a jumble of feelings, which were ultimately overshadowed by his trust that the God of his fathers had redeemed him: "From between the horns of the rams thou didst answer me!" (Ps 22.21; cf. Ps 31.5).

> Just like the psalmist, Jesus did not die in solitude, abandoned by God, but rather went to his death awash in a jumble of feelings, which were ultimately overshadowed by his trust that the God of his fathers had redeemed him.

Another interesting point centers on the repetition *'elî, 'elî*, that is, "My God, my God" (Ps 22.1). This cry indicates the depth of the psalmist King David's spiritual suffering and agony; but it also suggests that on the Cross, Jesus, when repeating these words, addressed the other two Persons of the Holy Trinity: the Father and the Holy

Stalked by death, the lonely David foreshadows Jesus' taste of God's abandonment of him on the Cross.

Spirit. A similar case is found in Exodus 34.6 where Yahweh, that is, the Word of God, appears to Moses in the form of a cloud and invokes the name "Yahweh" twice: "Yahweh passed before him [i.e., Moses], and proclaimed, 'Yahweh, Yahweh, a God merciful and gracious, slow to anger, and abounding in steadfast love and faithfulness....'" On the Cross, the Messiah invites the other two Persons of the Holy Trinity to share in the work of salvation that belongs primarily to the Son. Similarly, "in the beginning," the Father's creative work was shared by the Son (the Word) and the Holy Spirit (Gen 1.1–3).

Additionally, in verses 1–2 of Psalm 22, the use of the pronominal suffix "my" (a Hebrew grammatical device), found in the sufferer's invocation of "My God," shows the close relationship between the psalmist and Yahweh, and simultaneously, in the typological reading, between the Messiah and God. The phrase "Thou hast forsaken me" refers historically to David fleeing from King Saul (1 Sam 19.8–31.13). Stalked by death, the lonely David foreshadows Jesus' taste of God's abandonment of him on the Cross.

Surprisingly, the suffering Messiah finds enough energy to "roar" his question. The Hebrew term *šáagatî* means "my roaring" and designates a loud, strong sound, not a faint one, as many modern translations erroneously suggest by rendering this form as "groaning." The Messiah's question on the Cross resembles the sound of a

The Crucifixion, Nikola Sarić.

lion, a common biblical metaphor for Yahweh (cf. Judg 14.5; Is 15.5; Jer 2.15; Am 3.4, 8). In Hosea 11.10, as in other parts of the Old Testament, God is likened to a lion "roaring," that is, summoning the scattered Israelites through the strength of his voice. In this light, Psalm 22.1–2 describes the Messiah as a suffering human, yet strong, divine, and able to overcome the critical moment in his Passion, both bodily and spiritually.

Crucifixion, Armenian Hymnal

Accordingly, when they record Jesus' last hours on the Cross, the Synoptic evangelists unanimously underscore the fact that "He cried with a loud voice" (Mt 27.46; Mk 15.34; Lk 23.46). Christ, though suffering, is still the Son of the eternal God, and as God, he "roars" in his effort to summon his children to salvation. Christ's words, though words of agony, are also words of hope.

## POIGNANT SILENCE

> *Beholding her own lamb led to the slaughter, Mary followed with the other women, in distress and crying out: Where dost thou go, my child? Why dost thou run so swift a course? Surely there is not another wedding in Cana to which thou now hastenest to change water into wine? Shall I come with thee, my child, or shall I wait for thee? Give me a word, for thou art the Word. Do not pass me by in silence, for thou didst keep me pure.*
>
> – Holy Friday, Canon, 5th Canticle, Ikos

> *Today the undefiled Virgin sees thee suspended upon the Cross, O Word. She laments within herself and is sorely pierced in her heart. She groans in agony from the depth of her soul. She pulls her hair and cheeks, beating her chest and crying pitifully: Woe is me, my divine Son! Woe is me, Light of the world, Lamb of God! Why hast thou departed from before my eyes?… Where is the beauty of thy countenance? I cannot bear to see thee unjustly crucified.*
>
> – Holy Friday, Vespers, Tone 2

Throughout the centuries, Christian biblical interpreters and theologians have struggled to find the most satisfying explanation of Christ's cry of abandonment. How could Christ, the incarnate Logos, be forsaken by his Father?

In answer to this enigmatic question, Blessed Jerome explains that Jesus suffered, while the Word, the second Person of the Trinity, was

Moreover, in that silence a sacred drama, the very drama of our salvation, was impeccably played out.

quiescent (dormant, silent). According to St John Chrysostom, Christ's words, though words of agony, are also words of hope; to this St Paul might also have referred when he wrote that our Lord "made prayers and supplications with strong crying and tears to him that was able to save him from death" (Heb 5.7). St Gregory of Nazianzus states another point of view, saying, "This does not mean that he was abandoned by the Father, as some believe it (so Origen)...but, as I said, he represented us. Thus, we were abandoned and then accepted and saved by the suffering of the One who could not suffer."

Psalm 22 witnesses to God and King, to Father and Son, and in some measure sheds light upon the crucifying silence that forever marks "Good Friday." Nevertheless, the Father's conspicuous silence, as recorded by the Gospel and as echoed by the liturgical hymns prescribed for Holy Friday, will always remain a great mystery laden with divine grace, for how could a merciful Father be silent while witnessing the pain caused by the Cross?

But there was silence, a crucifying silence, as if heaven had mercilessly shut its gates to a mother-in-despair's bitter lament and to a Son-in-distress's innocent question: "Why?" This excruciating silence speaks volumes about the Father's majestic yet long-suffering love toward his Son, who had the fortitude not to accept quick deliverance, so that he "might obtain a better resurrection" (Heb 11.35)—both his and ours.

Moreover, in that silence—as cold-blue as a wintery sky at the earth's Poles—a sacred drama, the very drama of our salvation, was impeccably played out by what we perceive as an austere Father in heaven and a submissive Son on earth. Yet, this drama ends in a shout of victory, a call to salvation, and the Son seated at the right hand of God, his loving Father.

## ABOUT THE AUTHOR

**Archpriest Eugen J. Pentiuc** is Associate Dean for Academic Affairs and Professor of Old Testament and Semitic Languages at Holy Cross Greek Orthodox School of Theology. An Albright and Lilly Fellow, he is also a Professor of Scripture at St Vladimir's Orthodox Theological Seminary. His academic publications include: *Jesus the Messiah in the Hebrew Bible* (Paulist, 2006); and *The Old Testament in Eastern Orthodox Tradition* (Oxford University Press, 2014).

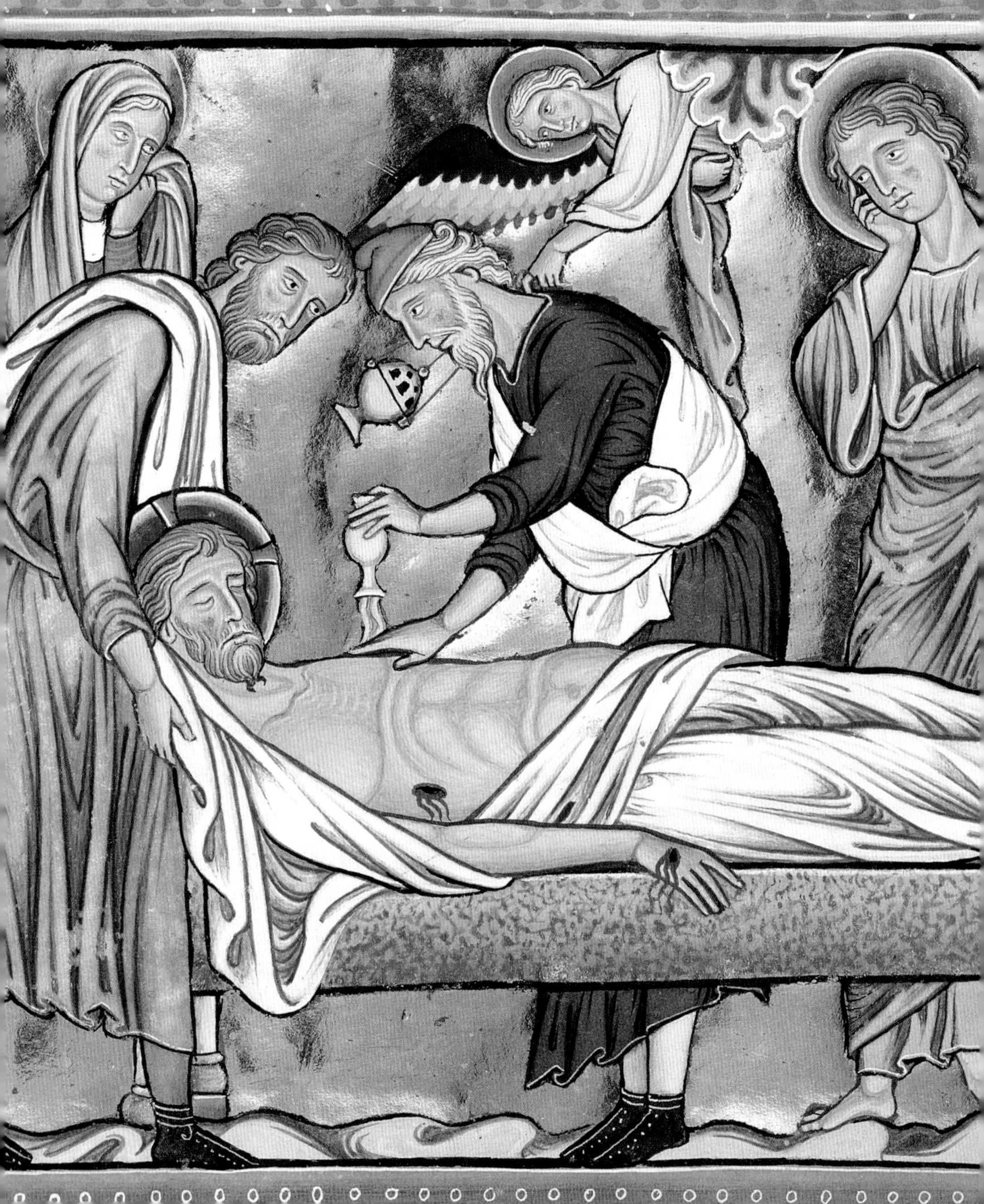

# HOLY SATURDAY

# 11

ARCHPRIEST CHAD HATFIELD

# Baptism and the Great Commission

*Baptism is Christian initiation. The goal of this process and its culminating rite is not some individualized, purely personal experience. The goal of baptism is initiation into a community of faith, a church. It is entrance into a way of life together, not a rite to do something to or for an individual in private. It asserts from its beginning that to be a follower of Christ means to be grafted into the body of Christ. There is no Christian without church, no faith outside the community of faith.*

> *Christian initiation and its attendant rite of baptism is the proper and primary business of the church. The church has been told to make disciples by "baptizing and teaching" (Matthew 28.19–20). Our major work is the evangelistic business of claiming people for the kingdom and fitting them for life in that kingdom. Baptism is that rich, multifaceted, complex way of engaging the body, head, and heart in that strange and glorious work of claiming, instructing, washing, anointing, blessing, and receiving people for the kingdom.*[1]

These words, written over thirty years ago by a Duke Divinity School professor, did as much to inform my theology of baptism as any other words that I have read, either while in or after leaving seminary. In truth these two paragraphs stand as the foundation for my own theological understanding of mission.

The Orthodox Church is in the business of making converts. The Great Commission, given by our Lord in the closing words of Matthew's Gospel, is not an option. Archbishop Anastasios of Albania has stated two remarkable tenets concerning evangelization: "A Church without mission is a contradiction in terms"; and "Indifference to mission is a negation of Orthodoxy."[2] I would expand this by saying: "A Christian not engaged in mission is simply not a Christian."

I am one of those people who are Orthodox by conviction. Like thousands of others in recent years, I made a choice to enter the Holy Orthodox Church, not counting the cost and believing that I had found the "pearl of great price" (Mt 13.46). I have not changed my belief that I was uniting myself to the Church of the Apostles. What I have done is matured in my Orthodoxy, to the point where I can now clearly see the need to rediscover, in most of the Orthodox Christian world, a new zeal for making the Great Commission central, once again, in our common life.

**A Christian not engaged in mission is simply not a Christian.**

For too many in Orthodoxy, words like "evangelism" and "outreach" are not claimed as our own and are given over to others. This sad fact keeps the "pearl of great price" hidden in ghetto worlds where cultural preservation and so-called "ethnic pride" is substituted for the "Gospel Truth." All too easily our faith communities have created a surrogate gospel supported by surrogate ministries that betray our baptismal identities as Orthodox Christians.

If we accept the dominical charge that we are to "go forth" to all nations, we will do well once again to consider the scripture readings and homilies on the Sundays of Great Lent: they are directed to those who are "preparing for holy illumination." This is true even in parishes where there are no candidates for baptism being prepared.

The Church is catholic and throughout the world we find catechumens seeking to be united to Christ and his Church. Great Lent is the baptismal season of the ecclesiastical year, and preaching must stir this memory and fill the faithful with zeal to share the treasure of their faith. The faithful are also called to listen closely to the prayers offered in the Liturgy of the Presanctified Gifts and to "pray for these brethren who are preparing for holy illumination and for their salvation."

The blessing of hearing and preaching directed to those preparing to enter the Church through baptism, chrismation, and Eucharist triggers the rediscovery of our own baptismal identity. We are called to once again recognize that having been united to Christ and to one another in Christ, we are his body. We have been sealed with the gift of the Holy Spirit, and we recall that this is not merely a past event, a static reality, but a "stream of living water" (Jn 7.38).

By privatizing the rite of holy baptism, we have separated the corporate nature of the mystery from the very people who are called to nurture the newly baptized. We have turned baptism into something precious for infants, and we have forgotten the radical nature of what it means to "put on Christ." The gospel is not only a belief, but a way of life, and, in this life, our values—the values of the kingdom—often find us at odds with the beliefs, values, and way of life accepted by the *zeitgeist*, the spirit of the age, which is passing and is not eternal.

We have turned baptism into something precious for infants, and we have forgotten the radical nature of what it means to "put on Christ."

If Orthodox Christians are once again to proclaim the glad tidings with boldness, we will need to restore the centrality of the Great Commission. We will need to bring ourselves to a fresh response to the New Testament teaching that we did not choose God but that he chose us (Jn 15.16). We are his hands, feet, and voice in this present world. Life in the kingdom involves our *synergia* in response to the love offering from God. We are invited to a conversion. We must become as little children to enter the kingdom (Mt 18:3).

Baptism of Christ, Claricia Psalter.

Many years ago I read a book written by Archbishop Joost de Blank of Cape Town titled, *This Is Conversion.*[3] I have never forgotten how "convicted" I was—to use an evangelical term—of just how radical true conversion really is. Try turning the other cheek when struck, and you will know exactly what I mean.

To go down into the watery grave of holy baptism is to rise to a radical, new way of life. Is this not why Jesus says: "If you have ears to hear, then hear" (Rev 13:9)? To hear the Beatitudes is easy, but to live the Beatitudes is radical to the extreme!

Baptism of Princess Olga, Sergei Kirillov.

This radical way of life that Christians willingly embrace is exactly what preachers are called to proclaim and to make clear to those who seek to unite themselves fully to Christ. To be signed and sealed with the sign of the Cross is to be marked as a Christian, and, come the dread day of judgment, an account must be given from one so marked. This is why a lukewarm faith—an anemic response to the great gift given in holy baptism—is so deadly.

This is true for us as individual Christians and corporately as the Church. A Church not engaged in mission is simply not the Church. A Christian not engaged in evangelism is simply not a Christian!

> Divine Liturgy on the morning of Holy Saturday marks the traditional time to baptize those for whom we have been praying throughout the Great Fast.

We who are members of the Orthodox Church make the audacious claim to have "put on Christ" and to possess "right faith and right worship." This is why we must be very conscious of our Lord's words as we live our lives as baptized Christians: "If I had not come and spoken to them, they would not be guilty of sin, but now they have no excuse for their sin" (Jn 15.22). I have been told, but I don't recall the source, that Protopresbyter Alexander Schmemann was once asked what the Orthodox Church needed in order to experience a revival. He responded: "Nothing, as we have everything needed. All we must do is begin to use what we already possess."

We have many positive signs that a recovery of the centrality of the Great Commission is underway. Many parishes have not only restored the prayers of the catechumenate, but they also have catechumens preparing for baptism and reception into the Church.

This year, as you celebrate the Divine Liturgy of St Basil the Great on the morning of Holy Saturday, be aware that this service marks the traditional time to baptize those for whom we have been praying throughout the Great Fast. The Old Testament readings from Genesis, Jonah, and Daniel are intended to be read at the actual time of holy baptism for the catechumens!

These readings then prepare us to hear St Paul in his Epistle addressing the Church at Rome with these words:

> *Do you not know that as many of us as were baptized into Christ Jesus were baptized into his death? Therefore we were buried with him through baptism into death, that just as Christ was raised from the dead by the glory of the Father, even so we also should walk in newness of life. For if we have been united together in the likeness of his death, certainly we also shall be in the likeness of his resurrection, knowing this, that our old man was crucified with him, that the body of sin might be done away with that we should not longer be slaves of sin. For he who has died has been freed from sin. Now if we died with Christ, we believe that we shall also live with him, knowing that Christ, having been raised from the dead, dies no more. Death no longer has dominion over him. For the death that he died, he died to sin once for all; but the life that he lives, he lives to God. Likewise you also, reckon yourselves to be dead indeed to sin, but alive to God in Christ Jesus our Lord.* (Rom 6.3–11)

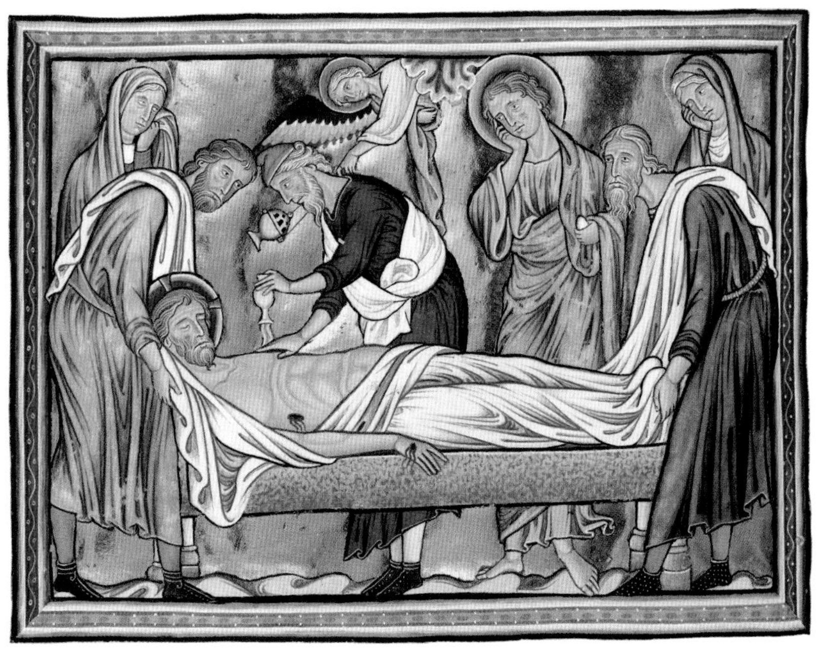

Entombment of Christ, Danish psalter.

Matthew 28.1–20 soon follows this Epistle reading. The Great Commission in the Gospel reading is placed at the center of the initiation rites for both the newly baptized and the faithful to hear, helping them to remember their own baptism and to give thanks to God for the gift of eternal life.

## ABOUT THE AUTHOR

**Very Rev. Chad Hatfield**, D.Min., D.D. is President of St Vladimir's Orthodox Theological Seminary, and the former President of St Herman Theological Seminary in Kodiak, Alaska. He has many years of pastoral experience in parish and missionary work, and continues to contribute to the fields of missiology and pastoral theology. He is the editor of the Orthodox Profiles and Orthodoxy and Missions series at St Vladimir's Seminary Press.

IC XC

# PASCHA

# 12

PROFESSOR RICHARD SCHNEIDER

# The Resurrection as Our Icon

*"No Cross, no crown!"*

William Penn's succinct formulation[1] reflects the core doctrine of Christian preaching, originally found in the words of St Paul (1 Cor 1.23–24) and reaffirmed without ceasing by Orthodox Christian preaching and teaching throughout the centuries. The Cross is essential and basic to our knowing Christ; it is fundamental to Christ's very nature, fundamental to our salvation.[2] However, St Paul ends his writing by reminding us that "if Christ has not been raised, then our preaching"—including preaching the Cross!— "is in vain and your faith is in vain" (1 Cor 15.14).

We first "see" the paradoxical mystery of Pascha in images of the *Anastasis*, which reveals to us the meaning of the Resurrection.

Orthodox worship acknowledges the Resurrection every single day of the year—including Good Friday, the day when the death of Christ on the Cross is especially singled out for attention. And no season more than Great Lent reminds us that our goal in taking up our Cross to follow Christ (Mt 16.24)—a goal kept firmly before our eyes by our fast—is Pascha.

These observations seem to present a dilemma. Where should we ground our hope of salvation: in the Cross as a *fait accompli*, or in the triumphant victory of the Resurrection?

It is tempting to think of Christ's death as the "payment" for transgression that frees us from the sin of Adam. And, it is even more tempting to think that Christ's Resurrection brings the atoning work of the Cross to an end: his "trampling down death by death" makes death null and void[3] and allows us "Orthodox"—"right worshippers"—to bask triumphantly in our assurance of heaven.

But if that were so, then why would we need Great Lent? Why do we start Lent with profound penitence, employing the Canon of Saint Andrew of Crete? Why do our liturgy, our preaching, the Scriptures, and Christ himself, constantly call us to repentance—to change?[4]

## A CROSS-BASED THEOLOGY

Clearly, a vicarious, commoditized notion of salvation in which Christ does our spiritual work for us falsifies the very idea of "putting on Christ." Equally clearly, a "two-step" historical viewpoint of first the Cross and next the Resurrection falsifies their inextricable relationship. Just as we recognize in Christ the seeming irreconcilability of a being who is a God-human, so too we recognize, in and through Christ's voluntary gruesome death, the seeming irreconcilability of the Cross with the Resurrection.

When the Orthodox Church urges us to "see" Truth with our physical eyes, the eyes of our mind, and the eyes of our heart—all working together[5]—it offers us more to contemplate than just the words of Scripture and liturgy. We first "see" the complex, paradoxical mystery of Pascha in images of the *Anastasis*,[6] which, more than any other iconography[7] reveals to us the meaning of the Resurrection.

Chora *Anastasis* fresco.

Let us examine this imagery in visual and theological detail, but before beginning, note that my use of the words "contemplate" and "examine" is not acci-

*Anastasis* illumination, Melisende Psalter.

dental. "Theologizing"—i.e., doing our utmost to think with the mind of God—through the medium of iconography is not a matter of awestruck, quietist mysticism. The common cliché about icons being "windows to heaven" through which heaven enters the world in transcendental radiance can actually lead us to spiritual harm (inasmuch as it identifies us as passive, vicarious beneficiaries of Christ's sacrifice).

Icons are texts, pictorial analogues to the Scriptures themselves.

Rather, icons are texts, pictorial analogues to the Scriptures themselves. Like the Scriptures, they require interpretation and exegesis before they will yield understanding to us. And, like all texts—especially the Word of God—icons call out to us, compelling us to read them to grasp the profound Truth they are teaching.

When we interpret iconography, the arrangement of larger figures and the depiction of smaller details do the most to reveal the icon's message. Any *Anastasis* icon is rich in such detail (see image on opposite page);[8] it would be fascinating to unpack all of its many layers: e.g., why are Kings David and Solomon, and John the Baptist always witnesses of the central event? But for now our Paschal reflection must be confined to the large, central image of Christ in hell, rescuing Adam and Eve, bringing them to himself.[9] In this figure, we perceive the heart of the doctrine being taught to us by the icon, and we visualize in the icon the liturgy which embodies its same message.

The *Anastasis* icon is not a mere illustration of a biblical text. Instead, it is a teaching tool, an assembly of images that presents the Truth of the Resurrection.

Our eyes are drawn instantly to Christ, the largest figure, placed deliberately at the very center, from where he commands the organization of the scene. He is shown in power, erect and firm, marking the central axis of the composition; his pose creates a symmetry that brings order even into the chaos of Hell. His exchange of gaze with Adam depicts St Paul's emphasis that Adam's salvation from death is a "free gift" (Rom 12.14–15). His forcefulness and power are manifested in the "trampling" pose of his feet, crushing the gates of hell, and with them Death/Satan himself, lying supine under Christ's feet.[10] His triumph over death is depicted not just as one historic moment but rather as an eternal definitive victory (1 Cor 15.57)—a rescue not just of Old Adam but rather of all humanity: "for as in Adam all die, so also in Christ shall all be made alive" (1 Cor 15.22). The Church has created and established this iconography as the identifying image of Pascha to visualize this fundamental Christian theme, thereby providing a visualization of the theological meaning of the Resurrection.

Neither the Gospels nor iconography recounts a historical narrative of Christ emerging from his grave,[11] and the icon is not a mere illustration of any biblical text. Instead, it is a teaching tool, an assembly of images (constructed in exactly the same way as our liturgy) that presents in one definitive image the totality of the Truth of the Resurrection—a Truth for all time, a Truth for us. The total experience of God in Orthodox prayer is strongly reinforced when we participate in Christ's Resurrection, simultaneously hearing the words "trampling down death by death" in song and regarding the icon with understanding. When we see Adam and Eve saved from the pit, we see ourselves.

*Anastasis*, Late Palaeologan period.

In the imagery of the *Anastasis* icon, Christ sustains Adam; Christ gives Adam strength with his right hand, while Eve prays and implores Christ in a well-known gesture of supplication. There is nothing gendered about this imagery; no misogynist intent in Christ holding only Adam's hand.[12] Not only Adam and Eve are saved from death by their dual act of supplication and acceptance of Christ's free gift. Rather, all of us

The trampled doors of hell have been re-arranged to form the Cross—hell's doors have become "the doors of paradise."

are in hell, all of us implore with Eve, all of us are sustained by Christ and saved by his Resurrection. The icon may not be a "mystical window," but it is certainly a mirror![13]

## ICONOGRAPHY AS A "MIRROR," NOT A "WINDOW"

In contemplating the *Anastasis* imagery, we realize that the rescue of Adam and Eve is far more than merely a personal gift to them, far more than Christ's recompense for the harm of their transgression. A closer look at the icon opens our eyes to the absolute inseparability of the Cross and Resurrection, giving answer to the theological question that prompted our meditation. Resurrection through the Crucifixion is everywhere in the lenten services—and indeed in all Orthodox services—and it is also everywhere in the icon.[14] Even in the highly narrative, story-telling design of our example (see p. 152), emphasizing Christ's power and reign, the "scepter" which he carries is the Cross, the wounds in his feet are prominent, and even the trampled doors of hell have been re-arranged to form the Cross—hell's doors have opened up to become "the doors of paradise."

This Cross-based theology of the Resurrection is made definitive by another version of *Anastasis* iconography, a rarer arrangement (see opposite page).[15] Here, instead of narrative power and manifest triumph, the central and dominant figure of Christ stands facing us,

*Anastasis*, from Mount Athos.

still and eternal; instead of grasping Adam, Christ holds out his hands toward us, and shows us his wounds. However, this visually shocking image of woundedness and death—which appeared first in the 11th century in a Gospel Lectionary as an illustration of Psalm 81/82.8[16]—is offered to us by the risen Christ!

At Great Compline, after reciting the Canon of St Andrew of Crete to show that our repentance, our supplication like Eve, is followed by the free gift of Resurrection, we sing that verse: "Arise, O Lord, and judge the Earth, for to Thee belong all nations!" (Psalm 81/82.8). Hell's doors have opened up to become the doors of paradise.

## ABOUT THE AUTHOR

**Richard Schneider**, in addition to his position as Professor of Hermeneutics and Liturgical Art at St Vladimir's Seminary, is Adjunct Professor and Co-coordinator at the School of Orthodox Theology, Trinity College, University of Toronto / Toronto School of Theology. He is also Emeritus Professor of Church and Medieval History at York University in Toronto, Ontario, and Emeritus President of the Canadian Council of Churches. He has served the Orthodox Church of America on the Metropolitan Council, the Preconciliar Commission, and the Council of the Archdiocese of Canada.

# 13

ARCHPRIEST JOHN BEHR

# Behold: Dying We Live!

Pascha approaches: we should reflect once again on this crux of our faith, orient ourselves anew by the perspective that it offers, and enter afresh into its mystery. By his death, his voluntary self-offering in love for us, Christ has destroyed death and granted us life. We say such words so often that we frequently become immune to the stumbling-block and scandal that they present, and so overlook their implications for us.

By dying as a human being, Christ has shown us what it is to be truly divine: Lordship manifest in service, strength in weakness,

The question is: How we are going to die? By clinging to all that we think is ours, our own life and possessions, our own status or merit?

wisdom in folly. If he had shown us what it is to be divine in any other way (acting, for instance, as a superhuman god), we could have had no share in him and his work. The fact is that we are all going to die, whether we like it or not. The only question is: How we are going to die? By clinging to all that we think is ours, our own life and possessions, our own status or merit? Or by following him on his path to Golgotha, laying down our life in love for him and our neighbors? Living, yet still dying, or dying to live?

## THE WITNESSING BODY

By his action, by his shed blood and broken body, Christ has called us to be his Church. We like to use the language of the Church triumphant, the glorious body with a mission to bring the whole world within its fold and so manifest the kingdom of God upon this earth. And indeed this is our mission: Go and teach all nations, baptizing them in the name of the Father, and the Son, and the Holy Spirit.

But we must never forget that the glory of this body is one that is only seen by those whose sight has been trained to look upon the Cross and see the Lord of Glory. As St Athanasius put it, the more that the Lord is persecuted and humiliated, the more his glory and divinity is manifest...to those that have eyes to see. And this continues, he affirms, in those who now constitute his body, those who take up the faith of the Cross and willingly submit themselves to death, that he might live in them.

Such a one was Blandina, a slave girl—the epitome of weakness in the ancient world—who for her Christian faith was hung on a stake to be eaten by wild beasts. Spectators in the stands saw only another seemingly misguided fool dying for their entertainment, but those who struggled alongside her in the arena "saw in the form of their sister the One who was crucified for them." By her dying, Christ lived in her, so that she now lives eternally.

St Blandina, Sr Joanna Reitlinger.

## THE SCANDALOUS BODY

Let us never forget that this is the glory of the body of Christ, the Church, in this world, this is the life we profess to live, this is the inauguration of a kingdom not of this world. As we endeavor to extend this kingdom, we must of course strive to ensure

Women at the tomb, Danish Psalter.

that our behavior does not provide a scandal or stumbling block to others. At a minimum, we must hold ourselves to the highest standards of the society in which we live. But we must equally not fall into the error of supposing that so doing is enough for the body of Christ to be "in good order." As the body of Christ, we can expect to be a laughing stock, held in scorn and derision—let us never forget this, and let our abuse always be for the right reason!

Troubles such as those currently besetting the Church have done so from the beginning, and they easily can become an occasion for loss of faith, especially if we set our stock solely on the "good order" of this world. Indeed, one of the desert fathers of old warned that "in the days to come" one would scarcely find faith on earth, and the struggle to keep the faith in such times would be greater than any ascetic feat performed of old. Just as such troubles can be an occasion for despair, so also can they be a powerful impetus, making sure that our focus is properly oriented, that our faith is in Christ alone.

We live straining towards the future, the Coming Christ, nourished by the hope he offers. Let us not then be weighed down by today's cares, for they too will pass; let us instead prepare ourselves for the still greater struggles ahead. We can only do this if our sights are truly set on the kingdom inaugurated by the Passion and manifest in those of us who by dying, live.

## LET US FORGIVE ALL IN THE RESURRECTION

Forgiveness is at the heart of the mystery of the Resurrection: "let us forgive one another so that we may cry aloud, 'Christ is risen!'" We cannot claim to be Christians, to dare to greet one another with this paschal greeting, unless we do so with a forgiving heart. But the depths of this forgiveness is not plumbed if we think that

> We cannot claim to be Christians, to dare to greet one another with "Christ is risen!" unless we do so with a forgiving heart.

Approaching Christ repentant & seeking forgiveness, our hearts will be broken so that the love and forgiveness of Christ can flow through us to others.

this means the repentance of others and our forgiveness of them, resulting in a peace, or rather a truce, that suffices us. Christ came to call the sinners, so that if we would be amongst the called, this is how we must regard ourselves, the chief, indeed, amongst the sinners.

We must be like the apostles: as Saul, confronted by Christ asking "Why are you persecuting me?" so becoming the great apostle Paul; as Peter, who before resuming his calling as a disciple, had to confess his love for Christ three times, standing by the burning coals, as he had denied Christ three times, warming himself by the burning coals. His experience harkens back to the vision of Isaiah who, seeing the Lord sitting upon the throne hymned by the seraphim, lamented, "Woe is me, for I am lost; I am a man of unclean lips," and so received the burning coal taken from the altar, hearing the words: "Behold, this has touched your lips; your guilt is taken away and your sin forgiven."

Approaching Christ in this way—ourselves repentant and seeking forgiveness—our hearts will be broken so that the love and forgiveness of Christ can flow through us to others. Then we will be able to receive, from the same altar and with the same words of forgiveness, the medicine of immortality, so that dying we also may live.

## UNLESS A SEED FALLS INTO THE GROUND AND DIES

We are called to take up the Cross, to die with Christ, *to become the one body of Christ*. Our divisions are truly a scandal of our own making; whether they are between persons, within an ecclesial body, or between ecclesial bodies, each and every one of us is responsible for our failure to make Christ present through our witness, our *martyria*, to a world that is increasingly alienated from God and increasingly thirsting for Christ.

Extreme Humility, Heather MacKean.

Clinging to that which we value—personal dignity, indignation associated with strife among ecclesial bodies, or pride in our distinctive ecclesial history—we are like the seed that remains alone, rather than the seed that dies to bear fruit. If we are to be Christ's one true body, we must follow him by dying to everything that separates us from him, to all that belongs to this world rather than to the kingdom; we must hold our-

selves open to wherever he may lead us. In dying, we might begin to make Christ manifest, for "dying" is how we "live" as his one body.

We are on the threshold of the Pascha of the Lord. This is not simply an annual event that we may forget once we stop singing "Christ is risen!" It is rather the eternal mystery present at every moment—every moment, that is, that we do indeed take to heart its proclamation and by dying, live.

## ABOUT THE AUTHOR

**Archpriest John Behr** is the Father Georges Florovsky Distinguished Professor of Patristics at St Vladimir's Seminary. His particular scholarly interests lie in the early Church, especially the development of theological reflection, asceticism, and anthropology—areas in which he has published a number of books, including: *Becoming Human*, and *The Cross Stands, while the World Turns* (SVS Press). He also serves as editor of St Vladimir's Seminary Press's Popular Patristics series.

# 14

ARCHPRIEST JOHN BEHR

# A Feast of Theology

As we approach Pascha, the Feast of Feasts, it is fitting that we consider once again the nature of the banquet to which we are invited. As we will sing at Matins on Holy Thursday, we are called to ascend, with our minds on high, to enjoy the Master's hospitality, the banquet of immortality in the upper chamber, receiving the words of the Word. The nourishment that we are offered is a feast of theology; the food that we will feast on is the Body and Blood of the Word, the one who opens the Scriptures to show how they all speak of him and provide the means for entering into communion with him.

The Three Hierarchs, Theodore Psalter.

Our chapel here at St Vladimir's Seminary is dedicated to Sts Basil the Great, Gregory the Theologian, and John Chrysostom. Although they each have a particular day of celebration, our patronal feast celebrates them together, as the Three Great Hierarchs. The hymnography for the feast celebrates first of all their words, their words of theology, how they spoke about God. The feast was conceived in the eleventh century as a feast of oratory: it was a celebration of those who found the words adequate to express the Word of God. Such theology is a sacred art—the Byzantines even called it a *mysterion*, a sacrament—and it is charged with divinity. It embraces and elevates the words of men to convey Jesus Christ, the Word of God.

The Church celebrates the Three Hierarchs as great examples of those who took on this work. Having studied at Athens and other intellectual centers of the ancient world, they used all their

God-given intellectual powers for the celebration of this divine task. If we too wish be disciples, or, more accurately, "students" of Christ, we must take on this task of theology, learning from and about Christ and being renewed in our minds. And there are two very important aspects of this that we always need to bear in mind.

## THEOLOGY BEGINS AND ENDS WITH THE REVELATION OF GOD

First, that theology is not an abstract discipline or specialized profession. It is not speculation about God himself, separated from his own revelation or what his revelation says about us. It does not take all the things that humans might think of as divine—omnipotence, omniscience, immortality—and then project them into the heavens. Such an approach would create nothing better than a "superhuman," with divine attributes, perhaps, but nothing more than the best we can humanly conceive.

Rather, theology begins and ends with the contemplation of the revelation of God, as he has shown himself to be. Anything else is not theology at all, but fantasy. We do theology when we contemplate God's own revelation: God, whose strength and wisdom is shown in the weakness and the folly of the Cross. Christ himself, the Word

Theology begins and ends with the contemplation of the revelation of God as he has shown himself to be. Anything else is fantasy.

Theology invites us to understand ourselves, and the whole of creation, in the light of God revealed in Christ by the Holy Spirit.

of God, demonstrates his strength and power in this all-too human way, by dying a shameful death on a cross, in humility and servitude—trampling down death *by death*—showing that true lordship is service. This One is the image of the invisible God: in Christ the fullness of divinity dwells bodily—the whole fullness, such that divinity is found nowhere else and known by no other means.

All of us, therefore, all of the people of God, must focus on the transforming power of God revealed in Christ by the power of the Spirit. As the Great Hierarchs affirmed, we cannot know what God is in himself, but we know how he acts. We are invited to come to a proper appreciation of the work of God in Christ by the Spirit. We are called to understand that Jesus Christ is indeed the Word of God, whom, by the same Spirit, we must convey in our words. To recognize him as the Word of God is not a matter of human perception, but to find the words to convey him certainly demands the application of our minds. It requires that we raise our minds to a proper theological level, that we may be transformed by the renewal of our minds. As Great Lent prepares us for the Feast of Feasts, so also honing our mental skills should prepare us for the feast of theology.

## WE CELEBRATE A PASTORAL THEOLOGY

The second point to remember is that the theology that we celebrate is a pastoral theology. The hymns for the Great Hierarchs proclaim that the pastoral power of their theology has overthrown the illusory words of the orators, of those who play with words, speaking on a merely human level. Their theology is pastoral, in that it shepherds us into true life. It invites us to understand ourselves, and the whole of creation, in the light of God revealed in Christ by the Holy Spirit.

Theologians presenting scholarship to the bishop, Fulda manuscript.

This is not simply a matter of asking "What Would Jesus Do?" Nor is it simply a matter of being "pastoral," as we often hear that word used today, in the sense of ministering to others on their own terms, enabling them to feel comfortable with themselves. Rather, it is the challenge to transfigure our own lives by allowing God's own transforming power to be at work within us.

When we are confronted with divine love in action, it is in the crucified Christ.

This means that we must confront our own brokenness, for this is how God has shown his own strength: it is only in our weakness that God's strength is made perfect. And we will only have the strength to do this, we only *can* do this, if we begin with God's own revelation, if we begin with the theology taught to us by the Great Hierarchs. We have to abandon what we humanly think divinity is, and we have to let God show us who and what he is. We must begin, therefore, with the God who confronts us on the Cross, who shows his love for us in the love that he embodies.

Reflect on this: that when we are confronted with divine love in action, it is in the crucified Christ. This reality reveals two things: how alienated we are from the call that brought us into existence, yet, at the same time, how much we are loved and forgiven. In the light of Christ, we can begin both to understand our brokenness, our emptiness without him, and also to be filled with his love. Theology shows us that the truth about God and the truth about ourselves always go together.

So, as we approach the Feast of Feasts, let us prepare ourselves to receive this revelation of God on his own terms. Let us prepare ourselves for the challenge his revelation presents, so that we might be transformed by this gift and, with renewed minds, find the words appropriate to offer the Word to others.

The Ascension of Christ, Nikola Sarić.

## ABOUT THE AUTHOR

**Archpriest John Behr** is the Father Georges Florovsky Distinguished Professor of Patristics at St Vladimir's Seminary. His particular scholarly interests lie in the early Church, especially the development of theological reflection, asceticism, and anthropology—areas in which he has published a number of books, including: *Becoming Human*, and *The Cross Stands, while the World Turns* (SVS Press). He also serves as editor of St Vladimir's Seminary Press's Popular Patristics series.

# Notes

## CHAPTER 1

1 Biblical commentators sometimes make a distinction between those raised who will again undergo a physical death, and those raised who have entered into everlasting life in a new "spiritual body," as described by St Paul (1 Cor 15.44); such commentators use the words "resuscitation" and "resurrection" respectively, to make this distinction.

2 John Chrysostom, Homily 10 on the Acts of the Apostles Translation taken (and modified) from *Nicene and Post-Nicene Fathers*, First Series, Volume 11, p. 63.

3 David Kid and Mother Gabriella (Ursache), *Synaxarion of the Lenten Triodion and Pentecostarion* (Rives Junction, MI: HDM Press, 1999), 109–110.

4 *Egeria's Travels,* trans. John Wilkinson (Warminster, England: Aris & Phillips, LTD, 1999), 58.

## CHAPTER 5

1 Vladimir Lossky, "Dominion and Kingship," in *In the Image and Likeness of God* (SVS Press, 1974), 225.

## CHAPTER 6

1 The Matins of Holy Thursday, a rich and beautiful service, is usually celebrated on the evening of Holy Wednesday. In many parishes in North America, however, the Service of Anointing is celebrated at that time, and the Matins service is omitted.

# NOTES

## CHAPTER 7

1 The word "eucharistic" derives from late Middle English: from Old French *eucariste*, based on ecclesiastical Greek *eucharistia* "thanksgiving," from Greek *eucharistos* "grateful," from *eu* "well' + *charizesthai* "offer graciously" (from *charis* "grace").

2 Text from the Divine Liturgy of St Basil the Great.

## CHAPTER 11

1 William H. Willimon, *Remember Who You Are: Baptism, a Model for Christian Life* (Nashville, TN: Upper Room, 1980).

2 Luke Veronis, *Go Forth*, from the Foreword (Ben Lomond, CA: Conciliar Press, 2009), 10.

3 Joost de Blank, *This is Conversion* (New York: Morehouse-Gorham Foreword Co., 1958).

## CHAPTER 12

1 *No Cross, No Crown*, William Penn, Jr. Printed in the Year 1669 (Wing/P1327). This first edition, written while he was imprisoned for religious dissent, carried the subtitle "In Defense of the Poor Quakers." In subsequent editions, Penn emphasized the Cross-theology of the phrase in his subtitle: "No Cross, No Crown: a discourse showing the nature and discipline of the holy cross of Christ and that the denyal of self and daily bearing of Christ's cross is the alone way to the rest a kingdom of God." [1682 and all following eds. (Wing/P1330)]

2 John Behr's subtitle of his work, *The Mystery of Christ: Life in Deat*h (SVS Press, 2006), beautifully captures this paradox.

3 St Paul does not make this fatal mistake: see 1 Cor 15.12–20ff.

4 See Acts 2.37–38, Romans 12.1–2, and Mark 1.14–15, and throughout the New Testament.

5 Ephesians 1.18. Cf. Georgia Frank, "Taste and See: the Eucharist and the Eyes of Faith in the Fourth Century" *Church History* 70 (2001): 619–43.

6 This name, usually written near the top of any version of this image, literally means "being again erect," i.e. "resurrection," and it is the only correct way to identify this image. The rescue of Adam and Eve by Christ, which forms the original iconographic core of the image, in many early examples is the only part depicted.

7 Any icon on any subject lets us "see" the Resurrection of the Crucified One, and through the eyes of the Resurrection we see and understand any icon (a matter for an entire book!). See

John Behr's discussion of the Crucifixion in the Rabbula Gospels (Fig. 1 in *The Mystery of Christ*), especially p. 28.

8 *Anastasis*, illumination on parchment, The Melisende Psalter, f. 9v; Egerton MS 1139, 1131-1143 CE, Jerusalem, monastery of the Holy Sepulchre / British Library.

9 This fact has frequently led to the misnaming of the Orthodox image as "The Harrowing of Hell"—a Western concept stemming from a medieval text, *The Gospel of Nicodemus*. Eastern depictions are always titled "*Anastasis*," indicating the true meaning of the event (See note 6).

10 This victory over the power of death is further revealed in our first image by the broken locks and fetters scattered beneath Christ's feet—a particularly clever way of showing triumph; the customary figure of Death himself, as a bound and fallen monstrosity under Christ's feet, reduces Death's power to absolutely nothing. The image derives from Psalm 109/110.1: "The Lord says to my Lord, 'Sit at my right hand and I will make your enemies your footstool,'" and even more from Psalm 90/91.13: "You will dwell on the lion and the adder, the young lion and the serpent you will trample under foot." See Ignatius IV of Antioch, *The Resurrection and Modern Man*: "in fact death has no meaning; it is pure absurdity, the very essence of non-meaning" (SVS Press, 1985, ch. 2, esp. p. 67). In the Paschal Troparion, Christ "tramples down death by death." The Song of the Three Young Men sung on Holy Saturday prepares us for this theme: "Deliver us in accordance with your marvelous works and give glory to your name, O Lord! Let all who do harm to your servants be put to shame, let them be disgraced and deprived of all power and dominion, let their strength be broken" (verses 20–21).

11 Behr, *The Mystery of Christ*, p. 98, is definitive. Although an image of Christ stepping out of his tomb is found in many Orthodox churches and late icons, this image is a borrowing from a Western medieval iconography. Traditionally, the Eastern Church never depicted an empirical moment of Christ's Resurrection, but rather presented images that challenged interpretation, e.g., the enigmatic empty tomb (Mark 16.5–8, the original ending of this Gospel) and fallen graveclothes; the Myrrh-bearing women likewise witness to proper understanding. For a detailed study of such early imagery and the eighth-century development of the present *Anastasis* iconography see Anna Kartsonis, *Anastasis* (Princeton: Princeton

University Press, 1986).

12 Indeed in many iconographic presentations of the *Anastasis*—especially in the familiar image from the Chora church in Istanbul—Adam and Eve are symmetrically flanking Christ, and he holds both of them by the hand. See Robert Ousterhout, *The Art of the Kariye Camii* (London: Scala, 2002), 78, fig. 90; and John Beckwith, *Early Christian and Byzantine Art* (Penguin, 1970; 2nd ed., 1979; new impression New Haven and London: Yale University Press, 1993), 318–319, fig. 280.

13 1 Corinthians 13.12: "Now we are seeing a dim reflection in a mirror; but then we shall be seeing face to face. The knowledge that I have now is imperfect, but then I shall know as fully as I am known." The standard metaphor for iconological seeing throughout Scripture and the Fathers is a mirror, and never a window.

14 See Ignatius IV of Antioch, *The Resurrection and Modern Man*, ch. 2: "Renewal Today," regarding our personal identification with Christ's Resurrection. This insight opens up another line of discussion that arises from the icon: we need to identify ourselves not merely with fallen Adam, but also with Christ whose right hand sustains fallen Adam! Christ supports but one hand; Adam's right hand—imitating Christ's right hand—is left for free response. This is why the Church reads Matthew 25.31–46 on the Sunday of the Last Judgment, directly before our Lenten renewal.

15 Anastasis from a twelfth-century Templon beam of Mt Athos, The Great Lavra, now in St Petersburg, The Hermitage Museum; see Helen C. Evans and William D. Wixom, eds., *The Glory of Byzantium* (New York, The Metropolitan Museum of Art, 1997) fig. 68B, pp. 120–22.

16 Kartsonis, p. 152ff and Plates 50 and 52.

# Images

## CHAPTER 1

Pages 12, 21

*The Raising of Lazarus*, 14th century, Byzantine, tempera & gold leaf on panel; Ashmolean Museum, University of Oxford, UK / Bridgeman Images.

Page 17

*The Raising of Jairus's Daughter,* William Blake, c. 1799-1800, tempera on canvas / Mead Art Museum, Amherst College, MA / Gift of Henry deForest Webster / Bridgeman Images.

Page 18

*The Raising of Lazarus,* The Hunterian Psalter, 12th century illuminated manuscript, folio 11v / Glasgow University Library.

Page 22

*Ernesta (Child with Nurse),* Cecilia Beaux, 1894, oil on canvas / Metropolitian Museum of Art, NY.

## CHAPTER 2

Page 26

*The Entry of Christ into Jerusalem,* from a series of Scenes of the New Testament, Barna da Siena (fl.1350-55), fresco / Collegiata, San Gimignano, Italy / Bridgeman Images.

Page 31

Detail, *The Battle of Novgorod and Suzdal (The Icon with the Miracle of the Virgin Orans),* ca. 1475 / Novgorod Integrated Museum.

# IMAGES

Page 32

*St Martin shares cloak with a beggar*, Prayer Book, including Office of the Dead, ca. 1430-40, Brabant / Walters Art Museum Manuscript w.164, fol. 163v.

Page 34

*The Temptation of Christ,* The Hunterian Psalter, 12th century illuminated manuscript, folio 11v / Glasgow University Library.

Page 37

*The Entry into Jerusalem*; Miniature from Psalter, Oxford, England; 13th century, before 1220. Source/ Shelfmark: Royal 1 D. X, f.4v British Library, London, UK / © British Library Board. All Rights Reserved / Bridgeman Images.

## CHAPTER 3

Pages 40, 48

*Joseph and Potiphar's Wife*, William Blake, 1803-05, pen & ink and watercolor on paper, / Yale Center for British Art, Paul Mellon Collection, USA / Bridgeman Images.

Page 45

*Mary Magdalene anointing Christ's feet and drying them with her hair*; Miniature from Psalter, Oxford, England, 13th century, before 1220. Source/ Shelfmark: Royal 1 D. X, f.4v British Library, London, UK / © British Library Board. All Rights Reserved / Bridgeman Images.

Page 46

*Christ Curses the Fig Tree*, Illuminated Manuscript, Arabic Gospels, copied in Egypt by Ilyas Basim Khuri Bazzi Rahib, who was most likely a Coptic monk, in 1684 CE. / Walters Art Museum Ms. w.592, fol. 58a.

## CHAPTER 4

Pages 52, 57, 61

*Abraham and the Angels*, Psalter of Ingeburg of Denmark, Ms 9/1695 fol.10v; c.1210, 13th century; vellum, French School / Musee Conde, Chantilly, France / Bridgeman Images.

## CHAPTER 5

Pages 65, 73

*Mary Magdalene anointing Christ's feet and drying them with her hair*; Miniature from Psalter, Oxford, England; 13th century, before 1220. Source/ Shelfmark: Royal 1 D. X, f.4v British Library, London, UK / © British Library Board. All Rights Reserved / Bridgeman Images.

Page 68

*King David Praying,* Greek Book of Hours, Late Byzantine & Gothic style, 15th century; may have been copied in Crete / Walters Art Museum Manuscript w.534, fol. 158r.

## CHAPTER 6

Page 76

Detail, *The Last Supper*, Axenti, Symeon, 16th century, fresco / Church of Archangel Michael or Panagia Theotokos, Galata, Cyprus / Sonia Halliday Photographs / Bridgeman Images.

Page 81

*Judas leads the multitude,* T'oros Roslin Gospels, 1262 CE / Walters Art Museum Manuscript w.539, fol. 190r.

Page 82

*Parable of the Banquet,* Nikola Sarić, watercolor on paper, 2014.

## CHAPTER 7

Page 89

*Adam and Eve,* Armenian hymnal, Constantinople, 1678 CE, by Yakob Peligratc'i / Walters Art Museum Manuscript w.547, fol. 99v.

Pages 90, 95

*The Last Supper,* Axenti, Symeon, 16th century, fresco / Church of Archangel Michael or Panagia Theotokos, Galata, Cyprus / Sonia Halliday Photographs / Bridgeman Images.

Page 93

Detail, *The Kiss of Judas,* 'Psautier d'Ingeburg de Danemark', Ms 9/1695 fol.25; 13th century, c.1210, vellum, French School / Musee Conde, Chantilly, France / Bridgeman Images.

## CHAPTER 8

Page 100

*The Last Supper,* psalter illustration; c. 1260, tempera & gold leaf on parchment, French School / Private Collection / Photo © Boltin Picture Library / Bridgeman Images.

Page 105

*The Kiss of Judas,* 'Psautier d'Ingeburg de Danemark', Ms 9/1695 fol.25; 13th century, c.1210; vellum, French School, / Musee Conde, Chantilly, France / Bridgeman Images.

Page 106

*Christ on the Cross and the Good Thief,* Titian, c. 1565, oil on canvas / Pinacoteca Nazionale, Bologna, Emilia-Romagna, Italy / Bridgeman Images.

# IMAGES

## CHAPTER 9

Page 111

*Peach Blossoms,* John William Hill, 1874, West Nyack, New York, watercolor and graphite on paper / Metropolitian Museum of Art, NY.

Page 113

*Jesus Washing the Disciples' Feet*, psalter illustration; c. 1260, tempera & gold leaf on parchment, French School / Private Collection / Photo © Boltin Picture Library / Bridgeman Images.

Page 114

*Christ Washes the Disciples' Feet,* Armenian Hymnal, Constantinople, 1678 CE, by Yakob Peligratc'i / Walters Art Museum Manuscript W.547, fol. 104v.

## CHAPTER 10

Page 118, 127

*The Crucifixion*, Nikola Sarić, watercolor on paper, 2017.

Page 124

*King David kneeling in penitence*, Grisaille Book of Hours, ca. 1460-70, Bruges / Walters Art Museum Manuscript W.180, fol. 200v.

Page 129

*Crucifixion*, Armenian Hymnal, Constantinople, 1678 CE, by Yakob Peligratc'i / Walters Art Museum, Manuscript W.547, fol. 107r.

## CHAPTER 11

Page 132, 143

*The Entombment of Christ,* 'Psautier d'Ingeburg de Danemark', Ms 9/1695 f.28, 13th century c.1210; vellum, French School / Musee Conde, Chantilly, France / Bridgeman Images.

Page 139

*Baptism of Christ*, Illuminated Manuscript, Claricia Psalter, Ausberg, German / Walters Art Museum Ms. W.26, fol.10r.

Page 140

*The Baptism of Princess Olga*, Sergei Kirillov, first part of the trilogy *Holy Rus*', 1993, Russian Art Gallery.

## CHAPTER 12

Page 146

*Anastasis* (wall painting) / Holy Trinity Greek Orthodox Church, Vienna, Austria / Godong/UIG / Bridgeman Images.

Page 151

*Anastasis*, ca. 1315–1321, fresco, apse of the parekklesion, Church of the Saviour, Chora, Istanbul (Turkey).

Page 152

*Anastasis*, The Melisende Psalter, f. 9v; Egerton MS 1139, 1131–1143 CE, Jerusalem, monastery of the Holy Sepulchre, illumination on parchment / British Library.

Page 155

*Anastasis*, Byzantine, Late Palaeologgan Period, Constantinople or Crete, second half of 15th century, tempera on wood, private collection.

Page 157

*Anastasis*, 12th century Templon beam of Mt Athos, The Great Lavra, now in St Petersburg, The Hermitage Museum.

## CHAPTER 13

Page 161

*St Blandina*, second century martyr of Lyons, Sr Joanna Reitlinger, ca. 1930, Paris, tempera on wood.

Page 162

*Holy Women at the Tomb,* 'Psautier d'Ingeburg de Danemark', Ms 9/1695 f.28, 13th century c.1210; vellum, French School / Musee Conde, Chantilly, France / Bridgeman Images.

Page 165

*Extreme Humility*, Heather MacKean, ca. 2008, Long Island, NY, egg tempera on wood.

## CHAPTER 14

Page 168

*Ss. Basil, Chrysostom, and Gregory the Theologian*, Theodore Psalter f. 35v: Additional MS 19352, 1066 CE, Byzantine, manuscript illumination / British Library.

Page 170

*Rabanus Maurus, accompanied by Alcuin of York, presenting his work to bishop Otgar of Mainz*, Fulda manuscript, 9th century, German School, vellum / Oesterreichische Nationalbibliothek, Vienna, Austria / De Agostini Picture Library / Bridgeman Images.

Page 173

*The Ascension of Christ,* Nikola Sarić, acrylic on canvas, 2017.

## COVER

*A Lily Entwined with Thorns*, illustration from 'Liber Floridus', Ms 724/1596 f.32v, ca. 1448, Flemish School / Musee Conde, Chantilly, France / Bridgeman Images.